Hotel Revenue Management

Hotel Revenue Management

The Post-Pandemic Evolution to Revenue Strategy

Dave Roberts

Hotel Revenue Management:
The Post-Pandemic Evolution to Revenue Strategy

Copyright © Business Expert Press, LLC, 2022.

Cover design by Charlene Kronstedt

Interior design by Exeter Premedia Services Private Ltd., Chennai, India

All rights reserved. No part of this publication may be reproduced, stored in a retrieval system, or transmitted in any form or by any means—electronic, mechanical, photocopy, recording, or any other except for brief quotations, not to exceed 400 words, without the prior permission of the publisher.

First published in 2022 by
Business Expert Press, LLC
222 East 46th Street, New York, NY 10017
www.businessexpertpress.com

ISBN-13: 978-1-63742-191-8 (paperback)
ISBN-13: 978-1-63742-192-5 (e-book)

Business Expert Press Tourism and Hospitality Management Collection

Collection ISSN: 2375-9623 (print)
Collection ISSN: 2375-9631 (electronic)

First edition: 2022

10 9 8 7 6 5 4 3 2 1

History is often shaped by small groups of forward-looking innovators rather than by the backward-looking masses.
—Yuval Harari, Homo Deus

Description

This book guides the reader from the building blocks of revenue management, to pricing science and merchandising, and to broader issues of setting objectives in support of a revenue strategy.

The discipline is evolving, and that evolution has been accelerated by the COVID-19 pandemic. Leaders in hotel revenue management, and more broadly in sales & marketing, need to understand this evolution, and lead and adapt accordingly. This will require a strong foundation in analytics—not just modeling, but also business analytics in support of a holistic strategy.

As more of the tactics of revenue management are executed through automation, and powered by machine learning, revenue managers will become more focused on strategy, and will need to think about revenue management in the larger commercial context of marketing, loyalty, and distribution. As the strategy component of the discipline increases, so too must the breadth of knowledge of revenue managers.

Keywords

revenue management; hospitality; hotel; pricing; strategy; analytics; business; optimization; goal setting

Contents

Foreword xi
Acknowledgments xiii
Introduction xv

Chapter 1   Context 1
Chapter 2   Building Blocks of Revenue Management 9
Chapter 3   Forecasting 15
Chapter 4   Inventory Management 23
Chapter 5   Pricing 27
Chapter 6   Discounted Rates 41
Chapter 7   Negotiated Account Rates 59
Chapter 8   Distribution and Loyalty 67
Chapter 9   Merchandising 73
Chapter 10   Total Hotel Revenue Management 77
Chapter 11   Revenue Management in a Downturn 81
Chapter 12   Revenue Management in a Recovery 91
Chapter 13   Machine Learning in Revenue Management 95
Chapter 14   Topline Analytics 101
Chapter 15   Talent 109
Chapter 16   Thoughts for the Future 113

Appendices 117
About the Author 121
Index 123

Foreword

The future ain't what it used to be.

—Yogi Berra

Revenue Management is at a watershed.

Hospitality Revenue Management had been rapidly evolving for the past decade as technology advanced and hotel firms became more astute about leveraging the vast amount of knowledge and data in Revenue Management practitioners and databases. The discipline was advancing in a steady, linear, and somewhat predictable, path.

Then COVID-19 intervened, completely disrupting the longest period of economic expansion the modern world has ever seen. Recovery from that economic devastation is just beginning, but the residual effect on hospitality is completely unknown, perhaps unknowable. The economy will not 'snap back' to a pre-COVID state. The only certainty is uncertainty.

Business travel demands are shifting as the pandemic has made millions of people in business much more comfortable with video conferencing and collaborating remotely. They may be slow to resume travelling as corporations extend budgets cuts. Discretionary travel, especially international travel, may be dampened by fear or legal restrictions such as certificates of immunity. On the other hand, there is a real possibility that travel will see a resurgence resulting from pent-up demand.

In this period of ambiguity, we need guidance. There is no script or playbook for the post-pandemic recovery, but thanks to Dave Roberts, we have assistance.

The title of this book, Hotel Revenue Management, the Post-Pandemic Evolution to Revenue Strategy, reveals the secret to success in the coming years. Revenue streams will continue to be unpredictable. It will not be sufficient to manage revenue, no matter how clever one is or how much technology is deployed to the effort. Strategies must be developed that will actively create revenue streams, not just manage the demand. Revenue Management must evolve to Revenue Strategy.

Any good book should challenge your thinking. A great read is one that validates your knowledge, but then, unexpectedly, it confronts you, perhaps uncomfortably. Do you really know what you thought you knew?

This book provides a penetrating analysis of existing Revenue Management thinking and practice. For me, it was a joy to see an experienced practitioner methodically dissect the fundamentals of Revenue Management—forecasting, pricing, inventory management and distribution. The book has a direct, no BS approach to what works, and what doesn't work.

More important than the analysis of contemporary techniques, this book describes the future of Revenue Management, which ain't what it used to be.

For years, the rigorous analytical approaches of Revenue Management began to find their way into other functions such as sales, marketing and distribution. Vast Revenue Management databases and experienced revenue managers would support these functions.

Revenue Strategy flips the script so that the analytical rigor and process of Revenue Management will not just support, but it will drive all decisions involving customer acquisition and retention. Revenue Strategy will be game changing, and it will be essential for success in the post-pandemic economy.

Indulge me a few words about the author, Dave Roberts. Dave is one of the unquestioned leaders in Revenue Management. Aside from the unique experience he has gained from his increasing roles and responsibilities at Marriott, he has earned respect from everyone in this discipline. I'm honored to be his friend.

His passion for Revenue Management permeates this book. The book is not a stiff and formal treatise. It's conversational. Reading the book was like being beside Dave as he grew and learned in the space. He shares his thoughts, and he even verbalizes his asides, so that the reader has the full benefit of his thinking.

Enjoy the journey with him. There is a lot to learn.

—Bob Cross
Chairman, Revenue Analytics
Author, *Revenue Management,
Hard-Core Tactics for Market Domination*

Acknowledgments

In the course of writing this book, I had the opportunity to work with and interview some outrageously talented business leaders, and top-notch academics, including three winners of the HSMAI Vanguard Lifetime Achievement Award (and likely some future award winners as well). Their wisdom and insights are reflected in this book, and I am enormously grateful to them. In alphabetical order, they are:

Chris Anderson, Professor, Cornell University
Brian Berry, Executive VP, Commercial Strategy, Pyramid Hotel Group
Jason Bryant, Cofounder and CEO, Nor1, an Oracle Company
Matt Busch, Senior Vice President, Equifax
Bob Cross, Chairman of Revenue Analytics
Dax Cross, CEO of Revenue Analytics
Sloan Dean, CEO of Remington Hotels
Craig Eister, Former SVP of Global Revenue Management & Systems, IHG
Cindy Estis Green, CEO and Cofounder of Kalibri Labs
Erich Jankowski, VP of Commercial Strategy, Host Hotels & Resorts
Pavan Kapur, Chief Commercial Officer, Caesars Entertainment
Sherri Kimes, Professor, National University of Singapore
Klaus Kohlmayr, Chief Evangelist & Head of Strategy, IDeaS Revenue Management Solutions
Mike Lukianoff, Data Science Advisor
Kelly McGuire, Managing Principal, Hospitality, ZS Associates
Juan Nicolau, Professor of Revenue Management, Virginia Tech
Andrew Rubinacci, EVP, Revenue Strategy, Aimbridge Hospitality
Trevor Stuart-Hill, President of Revenue Matters
Tim Wiersma, Founder of Revenue Generation, LLC

I'd like to thank Glenn Withiam, my supertalented editor, for all of his advice on this book. Thank you also to Business Expert Press, the publisher of this book, and a widely recognized leader in education for students and professionals alike. I am forever grateful to my many outstanding bosses, teams, and colleagues at Marriott, especially those in revenue management, but also to so many others, across several disciplines, at all levels, and all over the world. Please know that if I have ever worked with you, I have learned from you. And a special thank you to Bob Cross, recognized by many (including me) as the foremost expert in the world in revenue management, for his thoughtful foreword to this book, as well as his friendship and mentorship over so many years.

Introduction

Thank you for your interest in this book, and in this wonderful discipline. Revenue management is the love of my professional life, and I hope that passion becomes obvious to the reader. The purpose of this book is to share some things I've learned along my 25-year journey in the hospitality industry, as well as a vision for the post-pandemic future.

I'll make several references to the pandemic throughout the book. In fact, there is an entire chapter dedicated specifically to revenue management in a downturn, and another dedicated to revenue management in a recovery. While we all hope that COVID-19 will soon be mostly behind us, to far too many, the pandemic has been catastrophic, and often deadly. To a great many more, it has been unsettling in the extreme. To state the obvious, the global pandemic changed many aspects of our personal and professional lives. We will likely see that it changed the nature of revenue management itself. For example, we will certainly see an increased focus on cost containment and automation (true for the industry overall as well). That said, the pandemic has not changed and will not change many concepts and fundamentals, nor will it change the fact that the discipline of revenue management will continue its evolution to revenue strategy, which is the focus of this book. In fact, the COVID-19 pandemic has accelerated that evolution.

The book is geared toward revenue management practitioners at all levels and in all functions. Some practitioners may be new to revenue management, while others may have extensive experience. It is my intent that even the most seasoned revenue management experts, many of whom I am fortunate to know personally, will glean value from this book. In addition, my hope is that this book is useful for anyone in the hospitality business, not just those in revenue management. I firmly believe that a grounding in revenue management is essential for any leader in hospitality, regardless of job function or title, and I wrote this book with that in mind.

I hope this is also useful for students and teachers, as supplemental reading, as opposed to as a textbook. I'm hopeful also that parts of this book are useful well beyond the travel business, even though hospitality is my focus. Revenue management is a growing discipline, and is applicable to many non-travel industries, especially those with capacity constraints, from broadcast advertising to storage units to golf courses, and more. The pricing component of revenue management is of course applicable to virtually every business in every industry.

Although this book functions as a unified whole, it is structured in stand-alone chapters. Thus, it can be read end to end, or you can select specific chapters based on your own background and interest. Given the complexity of this discipline, each topic is inextricably linked to several others, making a logical flow of chapters a rather personal preference (this book reflects my personal preference). In each chapter, I will reference other related chapters, aiming to make it easier for the reader to follow, and connect the themes.

The chapters themselves represent concepts in revenue management, though many discipline issues cross multiple concepts. For example, channel distribution and alternative lodging are issues that involve several revenue management concepts, from pricing to forecasting to merchandising, and more. To the extent possible, I've kept the bulk of an issue within a given chapter. You'll also see that the topics of talent and analytics seem to permeate every chapter (that, by itself, is an important theme for revenue management), and each of these also has a dedicated chapter.

While I have tried to address the most important parts of this great discipline, there will necessarily be some omissions. As with any book of this nature, I had to balance scope with brevity. The content of this book reflects my own bias, specifically my above-property lens of revenue management, as this has been the focus of my career. My intention is to share a grounding in revenue management, and then to look ahead. I will share a vision for the future, and the steps we need to take to make that vision a reality.

I'm a bit of a hoarder by nature. I keep everything, including every notebook I've ever used in my professional life. The photo below shows several of them, from my time at Marriott, in chronological order, from 1996 through 2019.

INTRODUCTION xvii

Figure I.1 Notebooks from 1996–2019

In preparing this book, I reviewed all of my notebooks, looking for themes to include. In some cases, I was thrilled to see how much progress we have made as a discipline; in others, I was surprised to see that there is still much to be done.

Let's jump in.

CHAPTER 1

Context

What Does the Evolution to Revenue Strategy Mean?

Figure 1.1 HSMAI ROC, 2019

In June 2019, six months before we learned of the pandemic, I gave a keynote address at the Hotel Sales and Marketing Association International Revenue Optimization Conference (HSMAI ROC) in Minneapolis, Minnesota. The topic was "The Future of Revenue Management," and the theme of that talk was "revenue management will evolve into revenue strategy." The pandemic has accelerated this evolution, and that evolution is the guiding theme of this book.

"Revenue management will evolve into revenue strategy." That sounds like a bit of a platitude, so let me explain what I mean. First off, I am always careful about using the word *strategy*. It may not be the most overused word in the English language, but I believe it to be the most overused word in a business context. By *strategy*, I do not mean a business plan, a mission statement, or some lofty vision. I mean a path to differentiated results—a set of actions and decision-making guidelines that add value to the organization. A successful strategy is a recipe for success; this certainly applies to revenue strategy.

The evolution to revenue strategy, which is already underway, has some important implications. It means that the tactical decision making of revenue management will increasingly be done by technology, leaving the strategy work to us humans. The tactics of forecasting, pricing, and inventory management are quite well suited to modern technology, and we will certainly continue down that path. But the evolution to revenue strategy is more than merely a strategic approach to revenue management. I believe that the evolution underway is: tactical revenue management > > strategic revenue management > > revenue strategy. *Revenue strategy* is quite different from *strategic revenue management*, and we'll revisit this in future chapters.

At this point, I'd like to mention what some futurists claim to be the organization of the future: a human, a dog, and a computer. The human's job is to feed the dog, and the dog's job is to make sure that the human doesn't touch the computer! This is certainly an exaggeration, but the theme is real: computers will take on an increasing share of what humans currently do. I believe Andrew Yang has been right about this all along.

The portion of a revenue manager's day that is devoted to tactical decision making will certainly decline. The revenue manager will need to understand how their system works (if they have one), ensure that all inputs are valid, decide when to override the system, and understand the impacts of those overrides. The portion of a revenue manager's day that is devoted to strategy will increase. This means taking a holistic look at the topline revenue for a hotel or set of hotels, in a way that a computer cannot. It also means figuring out ways to get better at the tactics, including making wise choices for technology investment and decision-support analytics. And it certainly means setting the right goals, developing plans to achieve those goals, and analyzing and communicating progress.

There are many aspects of revenue management that I love. One is this: as a discipline, we continue to make meaningful progress each year. One can look back a few years and be quite impressed with how far we've come. I'm certain this will be the case many years into the future. For those of you that are now in revenue management, this may be the most exciting time to be in this discipline (pandemic aside for the moment), and I believe the same can be said next year, the year after, and so on.

What I'll share now are a few areas that require some attention for this great discipline of revenue management to evolve to revenue strategy; these were the themes of my talk at the HSMAI conference. The five areas I describe are, by necessity, only a subset of all of the exciting areas of revenue management. Each of these five areas (which I've lettered A through E) will be described in much more detail later in the book, along with several other topics that are critical to the evolution to revenue strategy. My intention here is to give a sense of where we are in this discipline and where we are headed. That said, the notion of "where we are as a discipline" is ripe for misinterpretation. To put a fine point on it, *we* aren't anywhere. Different organizations, and even parts of organizations, are at very different points in the evolution to revenue strategy. For example, as we'll discuss later in the book, the great majority of hotels do not yet have a revenue management system (RMS), and yet some organizations are pursuing the use of Artificial Intelligence to provide real-time pricing at the micro-segment level. However, regardless of where your hotel or organization is, my hope is that you will glean some wisdom from this following discussion, as well as from the rest of this book.

(A) Forecasting

One area that is in need of progress is forecasting. By this, I mean demand and supply forecasting in support of decision making, as opposed to higher-level projections, such as next month's Revenue Per Available Room (RevPAR). As an industry, we have put a lot of time and money into demand forecasting, and we have some of the brightest minds working on it, and yet ... we are not as good at this as we need to be. The tactical decisions of pricing and inventory are based on these forecasts (at least they should be). Why aren't we better at this? Partly, it has to do with focus. Forecasting is no longer a *glamorous* part of revenue management, and it can get pretty technical. We have significant opportunity to improve the science of forecasting, from the inputs to the modeling to the measurement. And the COVID-19 pandemic just magnified the importance of forecasting; as demand became less inherently predictable, the forecasting challenge got harder. Much more on forecasting can be found in Chapter 3.

(B) Pricing

Another area for improvement on our path to revenue strategy is pricing. There is a lot of opportunity in the field of *price optimization*, meaning the price recommendation engines that are a key component of today's RMSs. To be blunt, however, there is quite a lot of price optimization already in place that is being ignored. Really. Most RMSs today will recommend pricing, at least for retail rates (*retail* in this context refers to the nondiscounted rates for standard room types). Some RMSs go much further than that, as we'll see later. Based on many discussions with industry experts, as well as my own experience, these recommendations are overridden perhaps one-third of the time, and some of those overrides are quite significant in magnitude. Have we really built sophisticated price optimization software that is only used when it aligns with the user's intuition? We, as a discipline, can do better than this. We also need to expand price optimization to all segments and revenue streams, recognizing that this is a long-term effort. Much more on pricing can be found in Chapter 5.

(C) Total Hotel Revenue Management

Total hotel revenue management (THRM) refers to managing demand across multiple revenue streams. In its simplest form, it means managing transient, group, and local catering demand for both sleeping rooms and function space. More advanced THRM involves more revenue streams such as restaurants, outlets, and spas. Revenue management professionals, and others, have been talking about THRM for well over a decade, in some cases, much longer. Several surveys suggest that this has been identified by many as a significant opportunity for many years. THRM makes sense intuitively, and many companies have invested significant time and money into this. And yet ... despite some pockets of progress, we as an industry are not very good at this. This suggests some significant impediments. One impediment is objectives. For example, if you believe that the goal of our hotel's restaurant is to maximize profits, but I believe it is to drive overall satisfaction with the hotel, and we are evaluated and compensated according to those goals, then we will surely not agree on many decisions. THRM is also hampered by lack of decent quality data. While reservations systems and property management systems (PMSs) can provide a great deal of useful data upon which to make decisions, the same is not at all true for most F&B or Spa outlets, for example. You'll find much more detail on THRM in Chapter 10.

(D) Topline Analytics

One important step in the evolution to revenue strategy is for revenue managers to be integrally involved in *all* revenue decisions. This involves revenue management decisions with aligned-upon objectives, perhaps extending beyond short-term profit, as we'll discuss later. It also involves revenue management decisions for purposes of customer acquisition and customer retention (those pricing and inventory decisions could be quite different). And as hotels continue to develop more appealing features, revenue management must be involved in decisions of *demand capture*. For example, as hotels offer the ability to *choose your room* at the time of booking, this value could be captured in terms of a loyalty benefit, a channel benefit, a price increase, or simply a demand increase, to be captured with a combination of rate and occupancy. The revenue manager of the future will need to help guide decisions of the hotel/organization with a compelling narrative. The foundation, though not the entirety, of this guidance will be analytics, both decision-support analytics and performance management analytics. Much more on topline analytics can be found in Chapter 14.

(E) Talent

To state the obvious, talent is how you *win*. There are many facets of this, some of which I'll touch on throughout this book. Training in revenue management significantly lags the discipline. This is true all across the industry. Training, both revenue management specific as well as more general training for revenue managers, tends to be an after-thought in many cases. For the continued evolution to revenue strategy, we need a mindset of lifelong learning. We also need to bring in *external* talent into this discipline, with fresh ideas and new perspectives. However, I hear the following far too frequently: "I could never work in revenue management … you all just stare at a computer screen all day." Clearly, some PR is called for here ☺. In addition to bringing in external talent, we need to send our revenue management talent out and seed our respective organizations. I dream of a day when every leader in every discipline at every hotel, and every above property leader has a revenue management background! Much more on talent is found in Chapter 15.

These five topics are intended to give you a flavor of what's coming in this book and to provide structure for discussion of a complex discipline. These and many other concepts will be discussed, with some historical context and with a look to the future.

So, what exactly is meant by *revenue strategy*? As noted earlier, a strategy is a recipe for success; if it's not a recipe for success, it's not a strategy. Deciding what your organization is going to do is of course vital to success; deciding what you're *not* going to do is equally important, and often much more difficult. If you can't name some potentially worthwhile endeavors that you will *not* be undertaking, then you haven't made the tough tradeoff decisions and you don't have a strategy. I recommend using that litmus test anytime you see or hear the word *strategy* in any of your business discussions. Revenue strategy, then, means a recipe for success in revenue generation and capture. It does *not* mean revenue maximization, or even profit maximization (more on that in the next chapter). It is the set of decisions, based on clearly documented and broadly understood objectives, that determine how we spend our time and money. As Cindy Estis Green, CEO of Kalibri Labs, puts it, "strategy is really planning and resource allocation." While this of course applies to revenue management decisions related to pricing and inventory, it also applies *up-funnel* to all sales and marketing activities.

A coherent strategy is highly dependent on *clearly articulated* goals. . . I'll come back to this point in the final chapter. For now, let's note that these goals must spell out the desired balance between sometimes competing objectives, such as profit maximization versus customer acquisition versus customer retention and loyalty versus channel preference, and more. And yet, our language often does not support such clarity. In fact, in my view, our language has gotten *lazy*. How many of you have read an article about revenue management that describes the need to *maximize revenues and profits*? With my apologies to anyone who has ever written that, this is lazy wording! Maximizing revenues and profits is a nonstarter; you can maximize one or the other, but not both (with hypothetical exceptions that do not exist in the real world). An analogy would be the desire to *maximize rate and occupancy*. Both are desirable, but maximizing one means not maximizing the other. There are plenty of other examples of lazy wording. I mention this here, with a few examples, because wording reflects thinking, and lazy thinking will not move us toward revenue strategy. I hereby beseech anyone in hospitality sales and marketing (certainly including revenue management) to stop saying: *future data* (there is no such thing, nor can one be *over-reliant on historical data*, since all data are historical; if you mean forecast, kindly say "forecast" ☺—details are in Chapter 3), *understand market dynamics* (a common, but useless, platitude), *optimal profitability* (too vague), *healthy mix of business* (I don't know what to say here), *optimize our channels* (another useless platitude). While I'm on the topic of lazy wording, I cringe when I hear anyone refer to *revenue management data* or *revenue management numbers*, usually in reference to some topline metric such as RevPAR Index (RPI). If you hear this, it is likely from someone who doesn't really understand revenue management or even revenue generation. In the summer of 2020, I read three textbooks on hospitality, looking for ideas to incorporate into my classes; one book describes the role of a revenue manager as "responsible for making decisions that *optimize* [emphasis is mine] a hotel's RevPAR." Is optimize the same as maximize here? If so, say it; if not, describe why not. Given my background in Operations Research, I take *optimize* and *optimal* quite literally. These words are so often misused in business that I think we'd all be well served to avoid saying *optimize* and *optimal* unless we have a specific objective function and well-defined constraints. By the way, the same textbook says, "the revenue manager is responsible for maximizing occupancy and rate." Oh my. In the summer of 2021, I took a few online courses, and learned in one of them that the goal of a revenue manager is to "sell every room every night at the optimal price." In addition to being lazy wording, this one is also quite misleading. SMH (shaking my head). These particular examples are ones I've seen myself very recently and unfortunately fairly frequently, but there are plenty of others. Get your goals figured out first, then *clearly articulate* them to anyone who can impact them, and *then* figure out your recipe for success.

The role of revenue strategy at large organizations is ultimately the purview of the chief commercial officer (actual title, of course, varies by organization). Revenue management plays an important role, but all other topline disciplines are necessary for success. Operating in discipline silos, which based on my interviews is quite common in this industry, is an impediment to success. As Sloan Dean, CEO of Remington Hotels, noted, as we evolve to revenue strategy, the role of chief commercial officer will be reflected at all levels of the organization. Sloan predicts, and I think he is right, that we will see commercial strategy/commercial services leaders at the region, area, and market level soon—for example, an area director of commercial services could be an enticing job! I'll revisit this topic again in the final chapter of the book.

In conclusion for this section, let me say that the future of revenue management is in no sense predetermined. Rather, it goes in whatever direction we take it. I love this quote (often, but not exclusively, attributed to William Gibson), "The future has already arrived, it's just not evenly distributed yet." What does this mean? Every major step forward that we've seen for this great discipline was once merely a thought in someone's head. And many of the innovations and breakthroughs we will see in the next several years, including the steps to revenue strategy, are already in someone's head today—perhaps yours!

As a side note, let me add here that HSMAI puts on some great conferences, across many disciplines. And if you have an interest in revenue management, and haven't been to a Revenue Optimization Conference (ROC), I highly recommend it. The team at HSMAI is outstanding, and these conferences are really well thought out and structured.

CHAPTER 2

Building Blocks of Revenue Management

A Brief Primer on the Fundamentals of the Discipline

In the previous chapter, we discussed the context and motivation for this book, and described what the evolution to revenue strategy means. In this chapter, to get grounded, I want to take a step back and cover some basic concepts of revenue management. We'll describe what we really mean by revenue management, and review some terminology that you'll see throughout the book. Each of these basic concepts will be covered again in much more detail in later chapters.

Let's start at the beginning. What is revenue management? The discipline used to be called Yield Management, which was first used by the airline industry, and referred to using pricing and inventory levers to maximize the revenue yield of a flight or set of flights. Actually, the term "revenue management" is a bit of a misnomer. What we usually mean is demand management. Trevor Stuart-Hill, President of Revenue Matters, describes revenue management as "a business process designed to drive the financial performance of an asset through all market conditions." At a tactical level, hospitality revenue management is the science and process of making pricing and inventory decisions for the benefit of a hotel or set of hotels. Consider a "typical" hotel where we expect Sundays to be low demand, Mondays, Thursdays, and Fridays to be moderate demand, and Tuesdays, Wednesdays, and Saturdays to be high demand (this pattern is quite common). For example, a given hotel will charge a retail rate of $199 next Tuesday, and will only accept bookings for that day that also include a stay on the Monday before or the Wednesday after (so called "length of stay restrictions"; if Tuesday is expected to sell out, then these restrictions will prevent a guest from only staying on Tuesday, and will allow guests who also stay the day before or after). Or, the hotel will accept some lower-rated advance-purchase bookings for next Saturday, but no more than a predetermined number of rooms.

In the early years of revenue management, such decisions were made to maximize revenue. The role of a revenue manager, then, was to find the combination of price points and inventory controls that maximized revenue. As the discipline evolved, we began thinking more about profitability, recognizing that different revenue streams have different profit implications, and our decisions were (at least in theory) made to maximize profits, and the role of a revenue manager changed accordingly. More recently, our revenue management decisions are made to maximize "benefit"—mostly profitability, but also taking into account loyalty and channel impacts, as well as reactions of competitors. For those readers with a finance bent, you can think of this as maximizing the Net Present Value of all future profits (or future cash flows for you finance purists ☺).

These pricing and inventory decisions are based on a forecast. This forecast is a demand and supply forecast, as opposed to a revenue projection. The demand forecast is often an arrival forecast, broken down by rate "bucket" and length of stay. The demand forecast can also be a stay-night forecast, meaning a forecast of roomnights (RN), as opposed to arrivals. This is often used to determine "hurdles" to control inventory (more in a moment). The demand forecast is paired with a supply forecast, meaning: how many rooms do I have available to sell? This supply forecast is based on the physical size of the hotel, rooms already on the books (noting the specific stay patterns), out of order rooms, expected cancellations across all segments, and group attrition. Together, the demand and supply forecasts are the basis for pricing and inventory decisions. Chapter 3 covers forecasting in much more detail.

Pricing means putting "price tags" on the inventory, for each arrival date, length of stay, room type, and segment (and sometimes by channel). Some of this pricing is supported by price optimization software, and some is not (yet). Price optimization refers to mathematical modeling to generate recommended price points, details of which are in Chapter 5. For the segments of business for which we do not yet have price optimization, some combination of analytics and intuition is used.

The inventory management component is a bit more straightforward than forecasting and pricing. Inventory management is a math problem, or, more precisely, an optimization problem. With a given demand and supply forecast, and a given set of price points, the optimal mix of business for the hotel to book can be determined using some approaches from the field of Operations Research. Sometimes, a company or a revenue manager will knowingly make inventory management decisions that do not maximize profits, for reasons of loyalty or distribution for example, which we'll cover in Chapter 8. The nuances of inventory management for any given hotel can get fairly complex, especially in peak demand situations, and even more so in a hotel with multiple types of rooms to sell. An experienced revenue manager with sound judgment is critical. Details on inventory management can be found in Chapter 4.

Let me touch on two more fundamentals: Dilution and Displacement. I was at an International Air Transport Association (IATA) conference several years ago, and I remember one of the keynote speakers, from a major U.S. airline, saying something to the effect of "as a revenue manager, the most important thing you can do when you get back to work is to educate your sales and marketing stakeholders on dilution and displacement." The presentation was great, and the message is timeless. Let's briefly dig into each here.

What the airline industry calls dilution, we in the hospitality industry call, a bit more descriptively, tradedown. One of the fundamental principles of revenue management is to charge different people different prices based on their sensitivity to price. I highly recommend Bob Cross' seminal book, called "Revenue Management—Hardcore Tactics for Market Domination," which discusses this in detail. The two charts below describe this effect.

Both charts show demand as a function of price. For any economists reading this, you'll note that these axes are transposed (when plotting price elasticity, price is typically on the vertical axis and quantity is on the horizontal axis); I use this orientation here to more clearly demonstrate demand as a function of price. This orientation is also used later in the book when I discuss group pricing models, where the two major inputs are also a function of price. Figure 2.1 shows a single price point. At a price of $50, we capture 100 customers, and bring in $5,000 in revenue

12   HOTEL REVENUE MANAGEMENT

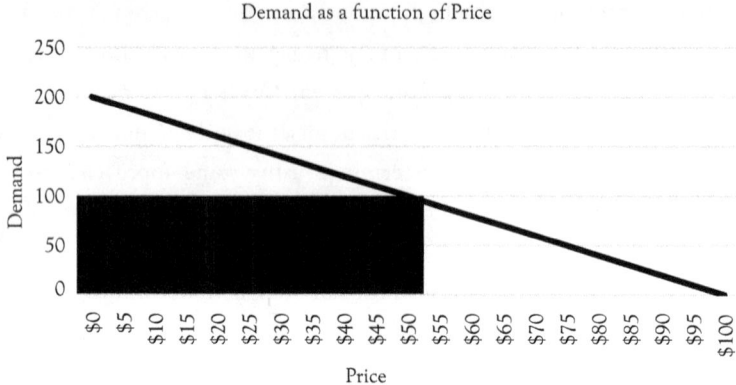

Figure 2.1 *Demand as a function of price: Single price point*

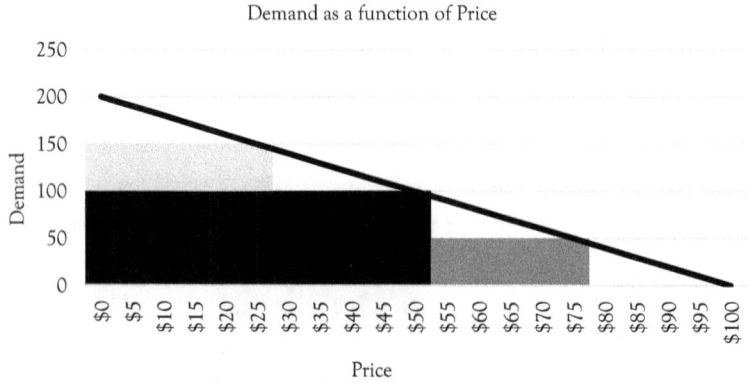

Figure 2.2 *Demand as a function of price: Multiple price points*

(the shaded area is $5,000). Figure 2.2 shows three price points. Now we can capture 50 customers at $75, another 50 at $50, and another 50 at $25, for a total revenue of $7,500 (represented by the combined shaded areas). Clearly, offering three price points is better than offering just one, as shown by the two shaded areas. BUT . . .

Consider the 50 customers who are willing to pay $75. How do we prevent them from paying less? Every customer who is willing to pay an offered rate, but who ends up paying a lower rate, represents dilution (tradedown). In this author's opinion, this may be *the most misunderstood* aspect of revenue management, and perhaps of all of sales and marketing. Much more on this topic is in Chapter 6.

Displacement can be interpreted as opportunity cost. If my hotel books a certain reservation, it may then forgo the opportunity to book something else. As an extreme example, let's consider my last available room. I have a customer who wants to pay $200 for it right now. But the value of that booking would not really be $200, because if I don't sell it now for $200, I can perhaps sell it to someone else, maybe for $200, or something more or less. Whatever I forgo represents the opportunity cost, or displacement. Displacement is dependent on demand levels (e.g., there is usually no displacement for a one-night stay on a low demand night because any booking will not preclude a hotel from taking another booking). Displacement is also dependent on the booking window. For example, a booking made on the day of arrival (meaning the booking is made on the same day as the guest arrives at the hotel) will have less displacement than a booking made a week in advance, all else being equal. The reason for this is that the opportunity cost of filling a room at the last minute is pretty low (such a booking would only displace another booking later that day). Finally, displacement is also a function of stay pattern; for example, a stay on a low occupancy Sunday night may incur a displacement cost if the guest arrived on the day before, because Saturdays tend to have high occupancy at many hotels. I envision a day when sales efforts are evaluated not on booked RN or booked revenue, but rather on revenue net of displacement. The value of a booking to a hotel, in terms of revenue, is the revenue booked minus the opportunity cost of that booking (meaning, revenue net of displacement). Displacement should be a part of *every* calculation of revenue impact, and one day it will be.

The reason that dilution (tradedown) and displacement matter so much, is that both need to be taken into account in any demand generation effort. For example, a promotion that generates demand for New York City in December, or Paris in June, will tend to have high displacement (pandemic aside for the moment), because the demand is already so high, and the opportunity cost of a booking in this case is that it tends to displace another booking. And demand generation efforts that offer discounted rates, as many promotions do, are always at risk of tradedown. Such promotions can be money losers even in low demand times (meaning that there can be significant tradedown even when there is no displacement). More on tradedown can be found in Chapter 6. In future chapters, we will also cover the impacts of loyalty and distribution on revenue management, which are critical and becoming even more so. We'll also discuss various analytics approaches and performance metrics to assess how we're doing.

So, there we have the fundamentals. If you have a good grasp of forecasting, pricing, inventory management, dilution and displacement, then you have a good grasp of tactical revenue management. The chapters that follow will take a deeper look into these, and other related topics, and will describe how they fit together in the evolution to revenue strategy.

CHAPTER 3

Forecasting

What to Measure, How to Interpret, and Why It Matters

In this chapter, we'll cover some key concepts of forecasting, including why we are not better at it. I'll discuss different measures of forecast error and which are appropriate under what circumstances, and even when forecast error doesn't matter (yes, I just put that in writing). I'll briefly discuss forecasting for meetings and events, and then close this chapter with a note on why forecasting is so important to the evolution to revenue strategy.

As noted in the introduction, the tactical decisions of pricing and inventory should be based in part on a forecast of demand and a forecast of supply. A strong demand forecast will (should) result in upward pressure on pricing, because with excess demand, I can tolerate a lower price conversion (meaning, a higher percentage of customers can say no to that price, and I can still have a high occupancy). Similarly, it is the forecast of supply and demand that drives inventory decisions, including the extent to which we overbook a given hotel. Virtually, every hotel *overbooks* to some extent. The reason for this is that, across the industry, perhaps 30 percent of booked reservations end up canceling or not showing up (this figure spiked in the early phases on the COVID-19 pandemic). Without overbooking, we'd end up with a lot of empty rooms; these decisions are based on forecasts. As an aside, a word of caution on overbooking: we must take into account the *cost* of walking a guest (meaning rebooking them in another hotel). In an oversold situation, walking a guest to the same brand of hotel a few blocks away, and probably making the stay complimentary and offering some extra points or credits, may not be too costly in terms of customer impact. But if the whole market is sold out, a walk becomes significantly more problematic. The most extreme case I've worked through was President Obama's inauguration in 2009. Hotels in and around Washington DC were sold out far in advance. We noted at the time that if we had to walk someone, we'd be walking them to New York City or to Raleigh, NC. As a result, there was effectively no overbooking! We did, however, require prepayment ☺.

If a RMS is in use, then a significant part of a revenue manager's role is to review supply and demand forecasts, and adjust when needed. This is particularly important around special events, when the system-generated forecast based on history may be less relevant. For an example of when a system-generated forecast based on history is less relevant, we needn't look any further than the impact of the COVID-19 pandemic. Transient booking windows were dramatically shortened, and demand was heavily impacted by travel bans, quarantines, and general health news for a region, each of which could change very quickly. Reviewing, and overriding as needed, a system forecast is also critical for hotels with significant group business. A revenue manager needs to determine how many rooms will actually be occupied for groups that are booked (e.g., it is not atypical for a given group to end up using only 85 percent of the rooms they have blocked). The revenue manager needs to work with their counterparts in sales and event management to determine how much of the room block can be *re-released* for sale. To make this problem much more complex, these supply and demand forecasts need to be done, and adjusted, by room type, and often by other attributes such as view type or other features.

As a notable aside, one fairly common statement after the outbreak of COVID-19 has been "historical data is useless, and we cannot use it to forecast," or some permutation of that. This is a logical absurdity. The only data that exists is historical data (as noted earlier, there is no such thing as *future data*). To ignore historical data is to ignore all data. The sentiment of the statement contains some truth however; the immediate future is not likely to look like the past during times of inflection. That said, any projection of any sort, provided it is not merely a wild guess, is based on some data or information. Even in the middle of the pandemic, any credible forecast of the future is based on historical data, albeit with some significant permutations to account for changes in booking windows, segments, source markets, or any other impact on customer behavior. As Kelly McGuire, Managing Principal at ZS Associates, says, forecasting during a pandemic is like "opening a new property in an unknown market."

One question that continues to trouble me, as well as several of the people I interviewed for this book: Why aren't we, as an industry, better at forecasting? What's holding us back? Part of the answer is, I believe, that forecasting does not get enough focus from the discipline. Any decent revenue manager can recite off the top of his/her head the RevPAR, RPI, year-over-year changes, and the corresponding figures for average daily rate (ADR) and occupancy as well. They can likely recite the mix of business by segment, perhaps even by channel and source market. They probably know the general stay patterns for their hotel by season. And much more. But if you ask a revenue manager, "what is your forecast error?" you may get a blank stare, partly because the question is not clear. I dream of a future where any revenue manager could immediately reply with something like "well, it depends on what you mean. For my hotel, the absolute transient demand forecast error from the system, weighted by booking activity, is 5 percent, and the system bias has been –1 percent recently, though both metrics have improved this year. The user forecast, however..."

I remember being a guest speaker at a well-respected university (name withheld on purpose). I was talking about a particular demand forecast model in place at Marriott. One student, presumably eager to impress his professor, raised his hand and asked, "what is your forecast error?" I replied, "it's 8 percent." He said "wow, that's high," to which I responded, "but you don't know what I'm talking about." I think I said it a bit more politely ☺. My point was that there are many different measures of forecast error. If I was referring to an aggregated demand forecast for the next month, 8 percent is dreadful; if I was referring to a daily arrival forecast by rate and length of stay, then 8 percent may be pretty good. In addition to the level of detail of a forecast, timing matters too. How is the forecast error weighted? It should be weighted by impact, meaning I care most during timeframes when I expect a lot of demand, and therefore, the pricing and inventory decisions that I make based on my forecast have the greatest impact. For example, I don't particularly care about my forecast error a month from arrival at an airport hotel (some exceptions of course), because any pricing and inventory mistakes will have little impact, given that there is relatively little demand a month before arrival.

Another consideration is *absolute* versus *bias*; both have important meaning. For example, my forecast may be too high on some days and too low on other days, but on average, for the month, it is spot-on. The bias here would be zero, meaning that there is no systemic over- or under-forecasting. However, if we count the magnitudes of both positive and negative errors (hence the mathematical term *absolute*), we get a sense of the true accuracy. Let's consider an example of a forecast that is fairly inaccurate, but is unbiased.

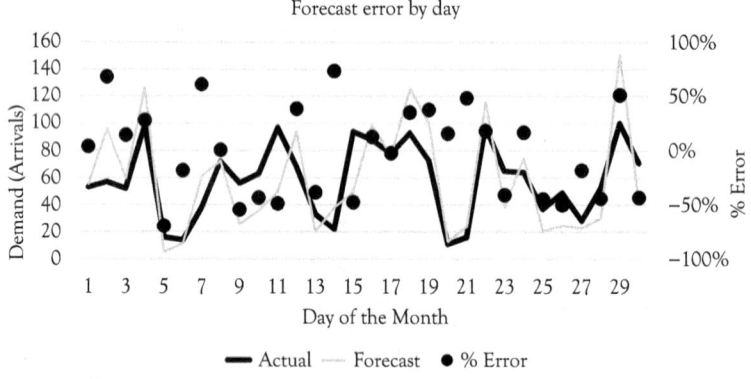

Figure 3.1 Forecast Error: Absolute vs. Bias

In Figure 3.1, the black line represents the actual demand by day, and the gray line represents the forecast for that day. For purposes of simplicity, assume each forecast was generated exactly x days before the arrival date. The dots, which line up with the secondary vertical axis on the right, represent the percent forecast error for each day. In this example, the average *absolute value* of the dots is 36 percent (average absolute percent error). But if we compare the sum of the daily values of the black line [1,758] to the corresponding figure for the gray line [1,754], we get an error of less than 1 percent; this represents the bias. It would be highly misleading to claim that the monthly demand forecast error is less than 1 percent. This is precisely why the distinction between *absolute* and *bias* in error measurements is critical.

For hotels that have some version of an RMS, we also need to consider the *system error* versus the *user error*. How accurate is the forecast from the system, and how accurate is forecast once the user has influenced it? Note that some systems do not let the user influence the demand forecast (which I think is a flaw), but even in these cases, the system versus user error concept still applies to a roomnight or occupancy forecast (sometimes called a *constrained* demand forecast).

In addition to increased focus from practitioners, and other stakeholders, there is opportunity to improve the actual science of forecasting. Evolving this discipline of revenue management will require using new and creative inputs to demand forecast modeling. The options are many. For example, if bookings at my hotel in Miami have unexpectedly spiked up, it may be that there was a corresponding spike in search activity a few days earlier, for my hotel or for the market. That search activity could have been on my own website, or on TripAdvisor, Google, or some other platform. If such a relationship can be established, it can be used to enhance our demand forecast—in this example, by using search activity as an input. Note that there are companies that provide this search activity tracking today; the challenge is how to incorporate this into an RMS to improve forecast accuracy. Search activity is just one example. Inputs to demand forecasts could include flight/travel activity, gas prices, consumer sentiment, changes in local demand generators, demand for nearby hotels, and much more. As an aside, the notion of using nearby hotels is not new; I refer the reader to a paper called *Attribute Smoothing—A Pattern Forecasting Technique*, on this exact topic, written (by me ☺) and published in 1998.

Another input that has yet to be used explicitly is supply of *alternative* lodging (*alternative* in italic because it is hardly *alternative* anymore). This flexible supply is also referred to as short-term rentals or housing rental services, among other names. How might this input help with demand forecasting? Today's RMSs use a forecast approach called a *time series*, in which historical demand is projected forward, with a variety of often complex permutations. An increase in alternative lodging supply will have a downward effect on demand for hotel stays. In this way, the effect of alternative lodging is seen implicitly in a hotel's demand forecast, meaning that slower booking activity will result in a reduced forecast. However, what if we could account for this *explicitly*? If an RMS, or an individual user, could directly forecast supply of alternative lodging, this could improve our forecast even before the effect was felt in terms of booking activity.

In addition to expanding the set of inputs, the science of forecasting is now benefitting from *machine learning*, details of which are in Chapter 13. While there has been some impressive work on the science of forecasting, much opportunity remains.

One often overlooked element of forecasting is an assumption inherent to most demand forecasting models out there: the independence of segments. What does this mean? Pricing and inventory decisions are based on a segment-level forecast. But that segment-level forecast is, in turn, influenced by your pricing and inventory decisions. This seems circular. For now, let's just focus on the inventory piece; the pricing part can be accounted for with a *price-sensitive forecast*, meaning that the demand will be in part a function of the price charged. The inventory piece can get tricky. For example, based on my forecast, I will take 20 rooms at the U.S. Government per diem rate, and then close it (make that rate unavailable). Once I close it, the remaining government per diem demand *may* book some other higher rate, perhaps even the retail rate. In this case, my forecast for other segments should change. The degree to which these other segment forecasts should change is directly related to the *incrementality* of the segment we just closed (please see the section on dilution/tradedown in Chapter 2, and the more detailed discussion of incrementality in Chapter 6). It turns out that the government per diem segment is largely incremental, meaning that if that rate is not available at my hotel, those customers are very likely to look at a different hotel as opposed to book a higher rate at my hotel. The reason for this is that the customer will only be reimbursed for the per diem rate, and anything above that will be at their own expense. One caveat to this is the portion of customers who book the government per diem rate but who are not qualified for it (so called *cheaters*; please refer to Chapter 7 for more details on this concept). But overall, this government segment is highly incremental. In the context of forecasting, this means that closing this segment will not have a significant effect on demand at other segments. The same is less true for other discounted rates; e.g., closing an advance-purchase rate is likely to increase, perhaps significantly, the observed demand for your retail segment (customers paying the retail rate).

Finally, it may not even make sense to track overall error, even at a segment level, weighted by booking activity, considering *absolute error* and *bias*. Why? Because these only matter *some* of the time. For example, let's assume I am forecasting demand to be 40 percent of capacity for some future date, and when the date arrives, the figure is actually 50 percent. That is a dreadful forecast error. But it likely doesn't matter because it doesn't impact the tactics of pricing and inventory. Situations similar to this example tend to occur around many holidays (high demand dates such as New Year's Eve in New York City, or Christmas week at Disney World, being notable exceptions).

All of the preceding discussion about demand forecasting is focused on transient demand. For us as a discipline to continue to evolve toward revenue strategy, we also need to make meaningful progress on group and catering demand forecasting. The opportunity and the challenge are both large. Some companies have made real progress in this space, but no one has nailed it. Partly this is because it is really hard. As noted in the previous section, we need to be concerned with demand as well as net demand (meaning inclusive of cancelations). The group segment adds another layer of complexity; unlike an individual transient booking, a group can *partly cancel*—this is known as *attrition*. As an example, consider a group booking for 100 rooms. On the day of the event, only 90 rooms are actually needed. The 10 *lost* rooms represent attrition. In some industry circles, this is also known as *group wash*. While we're on terminology, *slippage* refers to our estimate of attrition. In the preceding example, if the revenue manager believes that only 90 rooms will be needed, he/she may *slip* the group from 100 to 90, which impacts the number of rooms then available for sale to other customers. The challenge of group forecasting, then, is one of a demand forecast, a cancel forecast, and an attrition forecast, along with the timing of each (e.g., it matters quite a bit how far in advance a group will cancel, and how far in advance I can predict that happening). Much work remains in this space. Forecasting for meetings and events is a complex problem, and for this reason, it may be well suited to a machine learning approach (please see Chapter 13). There is likely to be some seemingly convoluted combination of factors that can provide some predictive value here. Such combinations of factors don't even need to make intuitive sense, they just need to help our forecast. In the context of forecast accuracy, we are in the business of prediction, not in the business of explanation. More details on THRM, which includes meetings and events, can be found in Chapter 10.

As a final word on forecasting, I'd like to share one of my favorite quotes; this one from Ian Wilson, a former GE executive: "No amount of sophistication is going to allay the fact that all of your knowledge is about the past and all of your decisions are about the future." To build on that, the connection between one's knowledge and one's decisions is forecasting! And the evolution to revenue strategy is dependent, in large part, on forecasting. We need to get better at it, *and* we need to spend less time doing it. Strategy work requires time and effort and applied brainpower. Reducing the time spent on tactical decisions, such as pricing and inventory, is predicated on automating many of these decisions. Such automation is of course dependent on an accurate, and trusted, forecast. Note that the generation of the forecast can be automated, but, at least for the foreseeable future the communication of that forecast requires a person. To put a fine point on it, an important role of a revenue manager is, and will continue to be, communicating a forecast to, and sharing forecast scenarios with, all key stakeholders.

CHAPTER 4

Inventory Management

Restricting What Is Offered for Sale, Why and How

In this chapter, I'll describe how inventory management works and provide a visual example. I'll then connect inventory management to channel management. I'll issue a caveat about the concept of *optimal mix*, and then close the chapter with a note on how this all fits into the evolution to revenue strategy.

Once you have your demand and supply forecasts, and you have set your price points across segments and room types, and maybe channels, you now must determine how much of each part of your inventory to sell, and when. Specifically, you *restrict* certain sales at certain times under certain conditions—this is why inventory controls are sometimes called *restrictions*.

To get grounded, let's consider a *very* simple example. My hotel has two rooms available for sale for each of seven days in a given week. There are 17 requests for that inventory, meaning that the *arrival demand* for that week is 17. Each of those 17 has an associated price point and stay pattern (meaning, which nights they want to stay). For simplicity, let's assume there are only two price points, $200 and $125, and that all stay patterns are either one or two nights. A visual representation of this type of demand pattern is shown in Figure 4.1.

We see that Inquiry 1 (Record# 1) is for a one-night stay on Monday, while Inquiry 4 is for a two-night stay beginning on Tuesday. In Figure 4.1, we see that Inquiries 1 through 7 have a price point of $200, and the remaining inquiries have a price point of $125. Note that this sequence is for viewing simplicity, as opposed to the order in which the hotel *sees* the demand. This hotel cannot accept all demand in this case; the reader can verify this by adding up each of the columns for SUN-SAT, and seeing that these days sum to a number greater than two, meaning that if we

Price:	Record#	SUN	MON	TUE	WED	THU	FRI	SAT
$200	1		1					
$200	2		1					
$200	3			1				
$200	4			1	1			
$200	5				1			
$200	6					1		
$200	7							1
$125	8	1						
$125	9	1	1					
$125	10	1	1					
$125	11			1	1			
$125	12				1	1		
$125	13					1	1	
$125	14						1	1
$125	15						1	1
$125	16						1	
$125	17							1

Figure 4.1 Inventory management—Demand pattern example

accepted all of the demand, we'd have more customers than available rooms. The inventory management problem, then, is to determine which inquiries to accept and which to turn away, with the added complexity that you don't *see* all of the demand at the same time, and you may need to turn away actual demand based on forecasted demand that may or may not materialize. Specifically, the problem is to maximize total revenue for the week, subject to the capacity constraints (in this example, two rooms available on each night). Note: for this highly simplified example, I'm ignoring any associated variable costs like housekeeping and commissions, and therefore aiming to maximize revenues as opposed to profits. I'm also simplifying the problem by not considering the weeks before and after our selected week; in reality, there will be *stay-throughs* from the prior week, and also from our selected week into the following week. The preceding example is just intended to give the reader a flavor of an inventory management problem.

So, what restrictions help us achieve our objective? I won't go through every step here, but let's get started. I'll say yes to Record #1, but no to Record #2 (the order of these two is not important here, but I want to restrict one of them). The reason I only want to accept one of these two inquiries, Record #1 or Record #2, is that I'd really like to accept Record #9 (or Record #10, but not both). Record #9 will bring a Sunday night as well, which I can accommodate; I'd rather have two nights at $125 than one night at $200 (again, for this example, I'm ignoring variable costs). To get to the specific restrictions to accomplish this goal, I'll need to think ahead. Once I book Record #1, I could immediately implement a *length of stay restriction* for Monday night; specifically, I will only allow a Monday night stay if it also includes a Sunday night. This restriction would deny availability to Record #2 but provide availability to Record #9. To continue through this inventory problem, I'll accept Records #3 to #8 as well. Records #10 to #12 will be turned away by simple capacity constraints. I'll accept Records #13 to #14, and then turn away the rest. This will result in total revenue for the week of $2,275. Note that there are a few different combinations that will get the hotel to $2,275, but none that will get higher (I encourage the reader to verify this ☺). It is easy to imagine how complex this inventory management problem can become, with many more rooms to sell, frequent forecast changes, forecast errors, varying lengths of stay, more price points, different patterns of stay-throughs, multiple room types, loyalty constraints, cancelations, early/late checkouts, and more.

The actual assignment of guests to rooms in a hotel is currently a very manual process. Jason Bryant, Cofounder of Nor1, envisions a future where we will have "real-time inventory management, where a booking immediately triggers a room assignment." He notes that humans can't do this, but computers can, provided that there is a clear objective function and corresponding constraints.

Some hotels also use price as an inventory control. If a hotel uses *day-based* pricing, where the price on a given day is independent of your stay pattern, then another way of restricting Saturday one-night stays is to raise the price for Saturday night.

A word of caution on inventory management: beware the notion of *optimal mix, at least in a broad sense*. It is often misunderstood. This concept can apply to segments and channels. Most people who work in and around hotels have heard some form of this concept, but I believe it is often (though not always) misguided. Let's consider an example: you may hear, "our optimal group mix is 40 percent." Taken literally, this means that 40 percent group mix is better than 39 percent, and it is also better than 41 percent. This is the nature of *optimal*. Despite the fact that this use of *optimal mix* is fairly common, it is absurd. If more group volume drives hotel performance, then we want more group, and if less group volume will allow for other more profitable business to be booked, then we want less group. This determination is (or should be) completely dependent on the level and the price response of demand *for each day across each segment!* Please refer to my comments on *lazy wording* in Chapter 1, particularly regarding the use of the word *optimal*. This is more than just semantics. The more an *optimal* figure, for group, negotiated account, contract, and so on, is put out there, the more likely it is to become a target, leading to perverse incentives (e.g., what happens if my hotel is exceeding its *optimal group mix*, and I have an opportunity to book a large profitable group?). The expression *optimal channel mix* has similar limitations, and yet, the concept is surprisingly common in the industry. One way to think about it: the notion of optimal can apply to specific dates but becomes much less meaningful *across* dates. With some notable exceptions, including Kalibri Labs, many in the industry still misuse the concept of optimal mix. OK, off the soapbox.

To close this chapter, I'd like to note that the evolution to revenue strategy is dependent in part on getting better at tactics. More precisely, this means getting better at tactics with far less effort (meaning more automation). Inventory management can be both tactical and strategic; as noted in Chapters 1 and 2, the former refers to maximizing profits, the latter refers to maximizing *benefit*.

CHAPTER 5

Pricing

Principles, Science, Strategy, and the Work in Front of Us

In this chapter, I'll give an overview of pricing across multiple segments, describe what is meant by *price optimization*, and provide some graphics to explain these concepts. I'll discuss how an RMS makes pricing recommendations, as well as the extent to which those recommendations are followed. Then we'll see how this modeling capability has expanded beyond the retail segment, as well as how much upside remains, and the work in front of us as we evolve to revenue strategy. We'll end this chapter with a discussion of how *demand-based pricing* is so often misunderstood.

Recall from Chapter 2 that one of the fundamentals of revenue management is pricing, and that this means putting price tags on your inventory. In practice, this means determining how much to charge for retail business, negotiated corporate business, weekend breakfast packages, wholesalers, advance-purchase, promotions, and many other rate categories. These decisions are made with some combination of art and science. If a revenue manager has access to an RMS that recommends price points, using price optimization, then he/she will use that as a starting point. Many hotels around the world, in fact the *great* majority (over 80 percent, based on some estimates from industry experts), don't have a system that recommends pricing. For those hotels, some combination of analytics and judgment is used to set pricing for every segment of business. As an aside, this represents an enormous opportunity for the discipline and the industry. A vendor that can figure out how to develop and sell a low-cost, easy-to-implement, simple-to-use pricing tool will meaningfully advance this discipline and industry, and also stands to make a *great deal* of money. Much progress has been made in this space recently. And such a system could be extremely beneficial to more complex hotels as well, even those that currently use a sophisticated RMS. As Bob Cross, Chairman of Revenue Analytics, notes, many RMSs of the past were designed and built with a user base in mind that had both the inclination *and the time* to do their own supporting analysis. Even for hotels that do have access to a sophisticated RMS, some *judgement* is still required. For example, an RMS may recommend retail price points for a given hotel, but it is the role of a revenue manager to validate these recommendations and to determine under what conditions to override these recommendations. Furthermore, even the most sophisticated revenue management software will give price recommendations for only *some* segments of business, in many cases, only the retail segment; for all of the other segments, pricing decisions are made based on analytics and judgment. While there is a great deal of analytics in place in support of pricing decisions across multiple segments, I believe that the future of pricing lies in price modeling and price optimization, for *every* segment of business. The RMS of the future will be much more sophisticated (more comprehensive models, more automation, more *self-learning*), and yet easier to use (more alerts and notifications, more *health checks*, less intervention).

To get grounded on terminology, I'm using the term *price modeling* to mean modeling the consumer response to a given price at a given time for a given hotel (think of price elasticity modeling—e.g., at $159, I'll get three bookings, but at $129, I'll get seven bookings). I'll use the term *price optimization* to refer to the recommendation engine that lives in an RMS; this engine uses price modeling along with demand forecasts and supply forecasts to actually recommend the price to be charged.

Price modeling capability has exploded in recent years, and for good reason. Many companies, certainly including Marriott, but also including other chains and several vendors too, have made great strides in price modeling. The concept is simple: if I charge $x, how many bookings will I get? The answer to that is based on modeling. Specifically, this means the relationship between a given hotel's price and booking activity, accounting for other factors such as overall demand level and competitors' pricing. Most of the focus thus far has been on retail rates, which may be the most straightforward. Let's look at an example:

Figure 5.1 shows a simplified view of a price response model (again with transposed axis orientation, as described in Chapter 2). For a given retail price, the model will predict the level of demand.

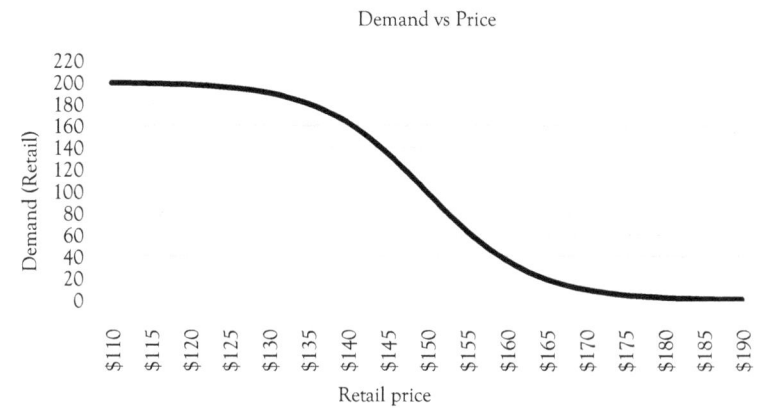

Figure 5.1 Demand as a function of price

A sound model will take into account any significant predictor of demand, the two most important being overall demand levels (based on season, day of week, recent booking trends) and competitive pricing (like it or not, demand for your hotel can be significantly impacted by the pricing of your direct competitors). This is depicted in Figure 5.2.

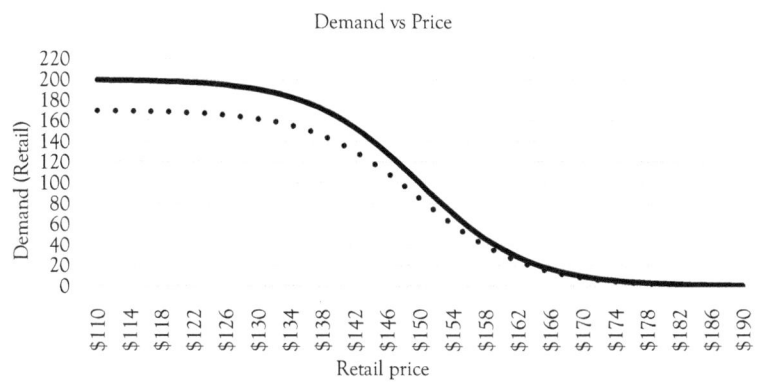

Figure 5.2 Demand as a function of price (input change)

The solid line is the same as the solid line in Figure 5.1. If there is some other impact to demand, for example, if a direct competitor significantly reduces its price, then the demand facing your hotel may look like the dashed line. Anytime that any meaningful input changes, the graph will change. Any model will need to be tested before it is implemented, of course. While it doesn't need to be perfect, it does need to provide predictive value, and this should be constantly validated. As the industry evolves, current models will lose some predictive power. For example, as more hotels offer some form of member rates, or channel pricing, the retail pricing models in place today will need to be updated. Similarly, cancelation/change policies and other fees will certainly impact a customer's response to a given price, and these too will need to be explicitly modeled, meaning taken as inputs to a pricing model.

There is a fairly common misperception about price response modeling and competitor rates; it goes like this: "why would I base my pricing on what my competitors are doing, when I don't think my competitors really know what they're doing?" At first, this may elicit an aha. However, that aha is misguided. Let me put this clearly: the prices offered by your direct competitors influence the customer response to your own pricing, *regardless of how those competitors' prices were derived*. In fact, the very definition of a competitor means that a change in their pricing will have an impact on the demand for your hotel, independent of whether the competitive prices were the result of sophisticated price optimization or wild guesses.

To state the obvious, such a price response model by itself doesn't bring any value. Revenue management software doesn't just *model* reality, it makes recommendations based on that model. What price should I be charging right now for a given date in the future? We want to consider the price response model for sure, but also underlying market demand, as well as available supply. Price optimization software does exactly this. Any time any of the inputs change, including how many rooms I have left to sell, the optimal price may change, and the price optimization software will reflect that.

Adoption

As noted in Chapter 1, adoption of system recommendations is an ongoing concern; across the industry, price recommendations are over-ridden perhaps one-third of the time. Why? The simple answer is that the pricing recommendations are not trusted. I believe that the crux of this is education and training, certainly for revenue managers, but also for key stakeholders. It is not uncommon for owners, general managers, and other important stakeholders to, knowingly or not, put pressure on revenue managers to make certain pricing decisions. Note: while in this chapter I'm referring specifically to overrides of pricing recommendations; the same concepts are quite applicable to overrides of forecasts or inventory controls.

Klaus Kohlmayr, Chief Evangelist and Head of Strategy at IDeaS, notes that "it is human nature to be skeptical of systems," but systems "can help take emotions out of decision making," which is key to revenue management. He believes that anyone involved in revenue management should have a grounding, formal or not, in micro-economics, in order to have the context to challenge system recommendations. That said, Klaus also warns of the "risk of over-dependence on automation," meaning that revenue managers will need to override the system on occasion, and must do so with confidence. He uses an analogy of airline pilots to emphasize this point: "pilots don't need to intervene. . . until they *need* to intervene."

There is a great deal of pressure on revenue managers, from numerous stakeholders (any current or past revenue managers reading this are now smirking at this understated truth). A focused effort on explaining how these pricing models work may alleviate some of this pressure. Revenue managers need to understand the software they are using, and the resulting recommendations. The system cannot be just a black box built by some technologists and statisticians. As an industry, we need to upgrade our training about the systems we use. And we need to make this training efficient; every revenue manager I've ever met (numbering well over 1,000) is extremely busy, and cannot devote hours per day over a matter of weeks to train on a system. With this time constraint in mind, customized training is in order. In my opinion, despite recent progress across the industry, this is an enormous need for this discipline. Every revenue manager should be able to explain how their system works, and understand under what conditions it should be overridden. And every system should have a supporting dashboard or reporting capability that demonstrates the frequency and impact of any overrides. I'm certainly not suggesting blindly following every recommendation coming from the price recommendation engine. But I am suggesting that whenever a revenue manager overrides a price recommendation, they have a reason for doing so, and that reason needs to be more than "it doesn't feel right." The reason should include some knowledge that the revenue manager has that the computer does not have. To state the obvious, *this presupposes that the revenue manager knows what the system does and does not know.* And the stakeholders (owners, GMs, and others) would be wise to ask their revenue managers about the frequency, direction, magnitude, and, of course, rationale for overrides.

At the same time, improving the models themselves will also lead to more trust, and therefore more adoption. This modeling effort cannot just be making existing models more accurate. In the broadest sense, a *model* is just a representation of reality. Reality in our industry is changing rapidly, due to changes in consumer behavior, growth in disruptors, changes in distribution strategy, and many other factors, and our modeling needs to reflect that. Clearly, we have much work in front of us.

Dax Cross, CEO of Revenue Analytics, noted "the first waves of Waze also had lots of skeptics." Dax's suggestion for users: "Flip the script. Instead of focusing on evaluation of outputs, focus on the quality of inputs. Focus on situations for which there isn't good data." For a hotel revenue manager, this suggests a higher incidence of overrides at inflection points in supply or demand. Such situations could include hotel renovations, new hotel supply in the market, new nontraditional supply, new rate types/offerings, or even inflection points in the economic cycle. Dax's point is more relevant now than ever; the COVID-19 pandemic presented an inflection, the magnitude of which was unknowable at the time. Overrides should have spiked up in the early phases of the pandemic; once the recovery becomes more stable and predictable, overrides should steadily decline. Tim Wiersma, founder of Revenue Generation, emphasized the need for safeguards, noting that "a system needs safeguards just as a human needs safeguards, and human intervention is critical to system safeguards."

So, what should the adoption percentage be? Overriding one-third of the recommendations seems too high, but the override percentage certainly should not be zero. The answer is, at the risk of sounding like an academic: it depends. It depends largely on the demand forecast accuracy of the system in place, but also on the accuracy of any price response models (including the quality of any shopped rates), both of which are hotel and date specific.

For illustrative purposes, a suggested goal for override percentage could be taken from Figure 5.3.

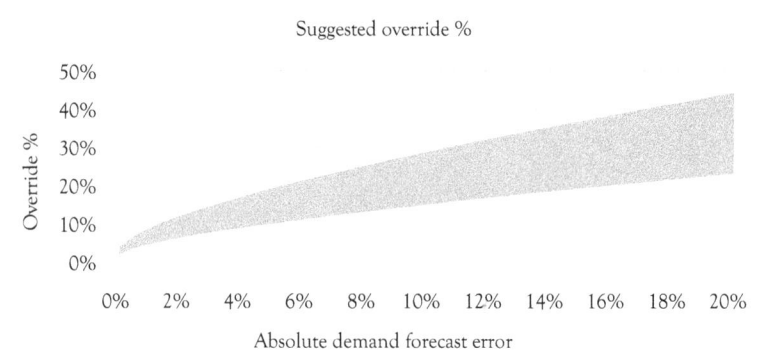

Figure 5.3 Override percent as a function of forecast error

The purpose of this graph is to demonstrate visually that hotels with lower demand forecast error should be the hotels that have a lower override percentage. The variation (the gray shaded area in Figure 5.3) is to account for other relevant factors, such as the quality, consistency, and frequency of rate shops. I believe that the creation of, and use of, a graph like this can lend some much-needed discipline to override decisions, and I recommend that revenue managers and their stakeholders use such an approach as a sanity-check for system adoption. Bob Cross, Chairman of Revenue Analytics, points out that "overrides should increase during economic inflections, when the user may know more than the computer" (referring specifically to the ability to forecast).

All of that said, in my view, an aggregated adoption rate of 90 percent should be a goal for the discipline overall, except for times of inflection. And in 2 to 3 years, when our modeling is better, that figure should be 95 percent. For some historical context, the following photo (Figure 5.4) is from a 2015 notebook (proprietary figures blacked out), when we at Marriott were keenly focused on system adoption.

We were interested in the adoption of our system pricing recommendations, but also on the direction and magnitude of overrides. Some of these metrics have been shared with owners and operators over the years as well. In addition to driving system adoption, these stakeholder discussions proved extremely valuable for the discipline.

34   HOTEL REVENUE MANAGEMENT

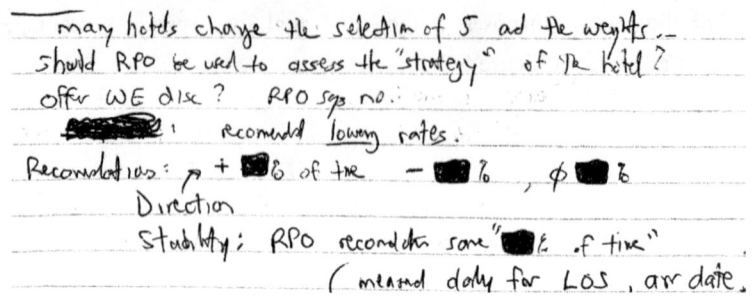

[Handwritten notes:]
> many hotels change the selection of S and the weights.—
> Should RPO be used to assess the "strategy" of the hotel?
> offer WE disc? RPO says no.
> ~~~~: Recommend lowering rates.
> Recommendations: p + ■% of the − ■%, φ ■%
>   Direction
>   Stability: RPO recommends same "■% of time"
>   (measured daily for LOS, arr date.

Figure 5.4 *Notes—Example of system overrides*

Beyond Retail

So far, this chapter has been discussing modeling for retail rates. Price response modeling should and will also be expanded to other segments beyond retail. Some companies, including Marriott, have made significant progress here. For example, Marriott's One Yield system provides pricing recommendations on premium rooms as well as for groups. I won't share anything proprietary here (sorry), but I can share a few thoughts. The price response model for groups isn't a *demand as a function of price* model like the retail model shown earlier in this chapter. Rather, it is a *probability of a given group saying yes to my proposed price* model, as shown in Figure 5.5.

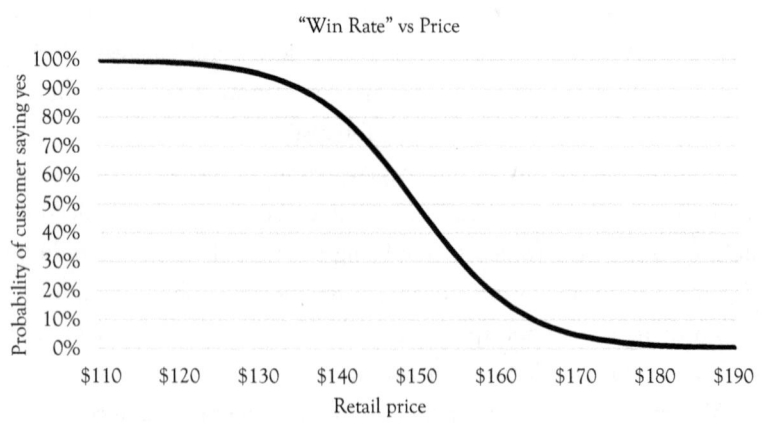

Figure 5.5 *Group price response*

The reason for this type of model is that we can record historical *yes* and *no* for every group inquiry (lots of data quality caveats here), as a function of price offered; this is possible, but quite difficult, for retail demand, as explained in more detail in Appendix 3. You may see these types of models called *win–loss models*; by contrast, the retail model described earlier is sometimes called a *win-only model*. Marriott's Group Pricing Optimizer (GPO) is described in the public domain. In fact, the team that designed and built it won the prestigious Edelman Award, given by the Institute for Operations Research and Management Sciences (INFORMS). If you Google *Marriott Edelman*, you'll see more details about this. Please note that Marriott's modeling work on premium rooms is not (yet) publicly available, so I will not go into any details here.

The evolution from revenue management to revenue strategy means that we will have price modeling on all revenue streams, including other segments of business such as negotiated rates and advance-purchase rates, as well as on F&B and outlet revenue. Getting there will require a commitment to this goal, and a plan to develop these new pricing models, as well as the recognition that this is likely to take several years.

While I cannot share any proprietary details about Marriott's modeling work, I will share an important learning about price response modeling: the models are generally *not transferable* across segments, an example of which I'll share in a moment. This is a *really* key point, and one that took me a while to fully appreciate. By this, I mean that, to the extent that buying and selling behavior is different across different segments, our modeling needs to reflect that. Without this context, the expansion of this modeling to other revenue streams *will* fail. And we need to appreciate that this modeling work is not primarily a math problem. The math part, while certainly not trivial, is solvable, especially with some trial and error, and smart people working on it. The harder part is taking a business problem and framing it as a math problem that can then be solved. This is really hard and requires a strong collaboration between revenue management practitioners and the model-builders, along with some creative problem-solving and stubborn persistence.

As an example of these models being nontransferrable, let's consider price modeling for negotiated account rates, a problem that, as of the writing of this book, no one has solved (for more context on negotiated account rates, please see the introduction to Chapter 7). A given hotel will want to know what price point to offer to a given account for the following calendar year; for simplicity of this example, let's assume it is a fixed rate all year. How could we model that? Can we just apply existing retail price modeling to this segment? Most assuredly not. The buying behavior is *very* different than it is for the retail segment. With negotiated rates, the first step is to get the travel manager approval, meaning that your rate will be *preferred*. But then you need to get individual travelers to actually book it. Any model will need to take into account the opportunity for rebids, as well as any changes by competitors, such as mid-year repricing. A model will need to account for the impact of last room availability, and the possibility of offering it or not, and pricing that *option* appropriately, details of which can be found in Chapter 7. A model for negotiated rates must also take in account the projected stay pattern of the account. For example, a more appealing stay pattern may warrant a lower price to increase the likelihood of a hotel becoming *preferred*. Such a model must also account for so-called *squatter* rates; these are rates that are account specific but not preferred or even negotiated. All of this modeling effort will require assessing the predictive value of past performance; for example, do some accounts tend to exhibit different sensitivity to relative price? Finally, the long-term relationship with an account may warrant pricing that is not profit maximizing in the short term; this could be because the account is also an important vendor, or because the account's business is critical during a downturn. The point here is that any expansion of price modeling is likely to require a significant effort and commitment, as well as a reasonable expectation of the timelines involved. In fact, it may be the case that the expansion of price modeling will not address negotiated rates in the near future. Revenue management leaders of the future will need to weigh the costs and benefits of price modeling for each segment of business, and prioritize efforts accordingly. Dax Cross, CEO of Revenue Analytics, points out that "negotiated rates may not be dynamic enough to even warrant a model," so it may be wiser to focus our efforts on segments that are more amenable to a model, such as extended stay. Craig Eister, former IHG executive, suggests that near-term modeling efforts should focus on defining the market rate more precisely (most retail models were built before the advent of so-called *member rates*). Craig also highlights the need for modeling work for room type differentials, view type differentials, as well as other attributes of the room.

Objectives

The further development of price optimization will also require a clarification of objectives. As noted in Chapter 2, the objective of revenue management has evolved from revenue maximization to profit maximization to something approaching long-term value maximization. For example, member or channel benefits certainly do not maximize profits, at least in the short term. For example, why would we upgrade an elite loyalty member when we have the chance to sell that room at a premium? Because we believe that this loyalty play will generate more value in the long term. The same can be said for member rates, meaning loyalty members booking on direct channels. These do not maximize profit in the short term. To complicate matters, the loyalty benefit may not go to the hotel that is generating this benefit. For example, an upgrade at one hotel may increase a customer's loyalty to the brand or portfolio, the benefit of which may well accrue to a different hotel. Knowing that, a given hotel may prefer to sell a premium room rather than upgrade a customer; the hotel clearly benefits from an upsell, while it may or may not benefit from an upgrade. Economists call this situation the *free rider problem*, and this is why chains and brands have upgrade policies in place, usually backed up by audits to drive compliance.

Benchmarking and Pricing

A word of caution on pricing: do not fall into the fallacy of over-interpreting benchmarking data as an explicit pricing diagnostic. This is frightfully common. In fact, I've even seen it in other published books and articles on revenue management. For example, STR data is extremely useful as a benchmarking tool. It is also useful for analysis of different performance drivers, for example, for use in A/B testing, for pricing, and other decisions. STR data (and reporting) represents an industry standard, trusted and used all over the world. The team at STR is top-notch, and I know several of them personally. The value they provide to the industry, and to academia, is monumental. In addition to benchmarking, STR data is useful for controlled experiments, or as a part of a performance analysis. However, this information is often not useful as a *standalone* pricing diagnostic, and yet, it is frequently used *precisely* that way. For example, if my hotel is gaining the ADR index, but losing the occupancy index and losing RPI, one could conclude that my hotel is overpriced, because it is growing rate versus the competitive set (often referred to as the *compset*), but more than offsetting this with a loss of occupancy versus the compset. Of course, it is possible that this hotel is overpriced. But it is also possible it is underpriced ... perhaps it has a strong occupancy premium without much room to grow, and should be driving average rate even more. There are any number of explanations for the observed results, only one of which is overpricing. Other explanations include renovations, segment/mix changes, location of demand drivers, and distribution changes. Furthermore, some segments may be overpriced, while others are underpriced; the same holds for different days or timeframes, and these nuances matter a great deal. To quote Albert Einstein, "everything should be made as simple as possible, but no simpler." Said another way, for the nerds reading this, the scientific principle Occam's Razor applies broadly but not in this case.

Competitive Response

What about pricing based, in part, on expected competitive reaction/response? I'm more inclined to raise prices if I have reason to believe my competition will do so too. This is a tricky topic, as there are some potential anti-trust concerns. That said, here goes ... virtually every aspect of business (and of life) involves decisions. We each make decisions all day, on a wide variety of issues, both personal and professional. These decisions have one thing in common: they are made in the context of other people making decisions about the same issues, and these decisions are most certainly not independent. This is at the heart of a branch of economics/mathematics called the game theory. As it relates to pricing, it is quite reasonable to assume that decisions by one competitor may influence decisions by others. In fact, this is not hypothetical at all; there is an abundance of research that says exactly this. For reference, you can Google *price war prisoner's dilemma* or something similar. The field of the game theory has plenty to say about price wars, and their severity and duration, based on a number of attributes. A detailed review of the game theory is beyond the scope of this book, but I strongly encourage the reader to become familiar with this field. To use foreign language analogy: if you are in a discipline that involves tactical and strategic competitive behavior, revenue management of course being a prime example, you do not need to be *fluent* in the game theory, but you do need to be *conversational*. As an interesting aside: it is fairly well understood that undercutting your competitors can trigger a downward spiral, and yet this is fairly common in a downturn. Why? Are we really collectively so stupid? I'll address this specifically in Chapter 11.

In addition to providing approaches to mitigate price wars, game theory can also be used to drive rates up. I'm going to refrain from putting many specifics on that point in this book; the obvious reason for that is anti-trust. In many parts of the world, we are subject to anti-trust constraints, and appropriately so. It is well beyond the scope of this book, not to mention beyond my own credentials, to offer advice related to anti-trust law. An abundance of caution, along with legal oversight and counsel, is strongly encouraged. Signaling future rates, with the intent to collude on prices, is almost always illegal. But the act of imitating competitor pricing, which is known in academic circles as *conscious parallelism*, is not. Conscious parallelism is generally legal in the United States, and the European Union, for example, provided that there is no *explicit* agreement among the competitors to do so. It is important to note whether conscious parallelism plays any role in decision making for your competitors (or perhaps yourself), and if it does, how you might use that to your advantage. Revenue managers with a strategic mindset will note that pricing decisions can be based in part on the degree of conscious parallelism in the market, and that this can be explicitly measured. To put a fine point on it: I'm more likely to raise my rates if I have reason to believe my competitors will follow, and I can assess that likelihood by evaluating their tendencies from the past. Important reminder: obtaining legal counsel is advisable in order to navigate the potential gray area between this and actual price collusion.

Demand-Based Pricing

One more point before we end this chapter: We should always strive for *demand-based pricing*, right? Of course yes, but ... this may be one of the most misunderstood aspects of pricing, particularly retail pricing. The idea is simple: pricing should be a function of demand. That is certainly true. The confusion comes in when people interpret this to mean pricing should be solely a function of demand *levels*. No! Let's consider a common example: Sunday nights at most hotels around the world. Let's assume my hotel is charging $200 on Sunday, but occupancy is typically 50 percent. I believe that lower demand warrants lower pricing, so I lower my price to $100. What happens? My hotel's occupancy grows, for example, from 50 percent to 55 percent, and I've just taken the lowest RevPAR night, and made it much worse! Retail pricing needs to be based on price response, and displacement. While it is true that Sunday nights have much lower displacement than other nights, this does *not* mean we should lower the price. Low season at a hotel does tend to have lower rates, but this is because of price response, driven by lower pricing in the market and in competing markets. The point here is that pricing should be based on demand (relative to supply of course), but this means the *elasticity* of that demand, in addition to merely the level.

I hope that one takeaway from this chapter is that the evolution to revenue strategy is dependent on advancing our pricing capabilities. And I hope that a second takeaway is that there is enormous opportunity to do so.

CHAPTER 6

Discounted Rates

The Most Misunderstood Aspect of Revenue Management

In this chapter, I'll cover some themes, and misconceptions, related to discounted rates. Specifically, we'll review the definition of a *successful* discount rate, as well as criteria for that success. Throughout the chapter, we'll use a hypothetical example of a college professor rate and discuss why that may or may not be a good idea, using the concept of *incremental* versus *tradedown* (dilution), introduced in Chapter 2, as a guide. We'll look at *price discrimination* and apply that concept to advance-purchase rates and to last-minute rates. I'll introduce a price discrimination approach that has yet to be implemented and reasons why it should be. And we'll end the chapter with measurements of success, including some specific approaches to evaluating a discounted rate. As noted in Chapter 2, I believe this topic of discounted rates to be *the* most misunderstood aspect of revenue management. As the discipline evolves to revenue strategy, and is involved in, and driving, all revenue generation decisions, we need a holistic and unbiased perspective on discounted rates. The COVID-19 pandemic certainly put a spotlight on discounted rates; in Chapter 11, we'll look at the competitive nature of discounted rates and how to avoid a *discount war* in a downturn.

Let's begin with a note on terminology: in this book, I'm using the term *discounted rate* to mean a rate that is below the prevailing retail rate. Some people use *discounted rate* to refer to a lowered retail rate, which I will not do in this book. A sound pricing structure for standard rooms will have a retail rate (for a given hotel/arrival date) and some discounted rates (see the two charts in the dilution and displacement section in Chapter 2 for why this is true). Of course, the retail rate for a given day will fluctuate for a variety of reasons, and there will be different retail rates for different room types. Let's work through an illustrative example.

Consider transient demand for a standard room for a given future date. Let's assume the retail rate is $150. We will capture some demand at $150, but unless we can fill all remaining rooms at that price, we may want to go after some more price sensitive demand as well, using discounted rates. Let's further assume that I only offer one discounted rate, and it is for college professors (in case the reader misses the reference, that group now includes me). Is this a good idea to offer this rate? For this illustrative example, let's ignore the fact that some professors are government employees and may qualify for a government per diem rate.

For a discounted rate to be a good idea, two things need to be true:

I. The rate needs to be either *fenced* or *qualified*. Fenced means that the buyer must *do* something to get the rate, such as pay with a certain credit card, or book two weeks in advance. Qualified means that the buyer must *be* a member of some group, and this discounted rate is only available to that group, and can be managed as such, usually with an online ID or proper photo ID at the front desk.
II. The discounted rate needs to be targeted to a more price-sensitive audience, meaning an audience that is more price sensitive than those buying the retail rate.

College Professor Rate Example

Let's consider a college professor rate, meaning a discounted rate targeted toward college professors. It is certainly not fenced (meaning, I can book it in any manner I wish). But it is qualified. Let's assume that every college professor has some easily recognizable ID to show at the front desk, or perhaps is given an online ID that allows him/her to book this rate. So, we can satisfy Condition #1. What about Condition #2? Are college professors more price-sensitive than the overall population? That's a tough case to make. The pay of a college professor in the United States, while too low (said with a self-serving ☺), is well above the median income, and even above the average of people who stay in hotels (people with low incomes tend not to stay in hotels very often). To make the case that this is a good idea, we'd need to show that professors are more price-sensitive than retail customers, meaning they have a different price elasticity.

DISCOUNTED RATES   43

Demand: Quantity vs Price

[Chart showing demand curves for Population and Professors, with Quantity on y-axis (0 to 1,000) and Price on x-axis ($110 to $190)]

— Population   • • Professors

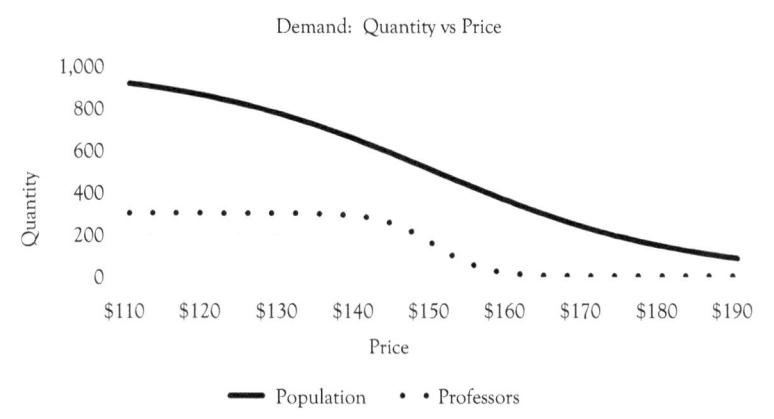

Figure 6.1 Example—Price sensitivity of college professors

Figure 6.1 shows what this would look like (once again with transposed axes). Let's assume my retail price is $150. If I lowered it to $149, my revenues would go up by 2 percent (I'll spare you the math here; it can be found in Appendix 1). I may not want to lower the rate, even though revenues would go up, as I need to consider profit. More on that in a moment. But what if I lowered the rate just for college professors? It turns out (again, the math is in Appendix 1) that lowering the rate to $149 for college professors would increase demand by 15 percent, and revenue by 14 percent (clearly an extreme example, for illustrative purposes). So, this is a case where lowering the retail rate may be a bad idea, but offering a discounted rate may be a good idea. Full disclosure: I don't know the price sensitivity of college professors as a whole, but despite the fact that such a rate would benefit me personally, I'm pretty sure it would be a money loser, because I doubt that college professors are more price-sensitive than the overall customer base. As an aside: I do believe that such a discount rate would make sense for elementary, junior high, and high school teachers, who are, in my opinion, woefully underpaid for the work they do, and by necessity, more price-sensitive.

More generally, here's a way to think about discounted rates; for simplicity, let's consider only transient rates, standard room types, and one-night bookings. Every booking at a discounted rate, at any hotel in the world, can be thought of in one of two ways: (a) it is *incremental* or (b) it is *tradedown*.

44 HOTEL REVENUE MANAGEMENT

To make the example more compelling, let's consider a college professor discount of 30 percent off the retail rate. We implement this at a given hotel, and we get 1,000 bookings (or 1,000 RN, given our assumption of only one-night stays) over the course of a year. Every one of those bookings is either a) incremental or b) tradedown. If it is incremental, this means that, without the college professor rate, we would not have gotten that booking. If it is tradedown, it means that if we didn't have the college professor rate, we would have gotten that booking at the full retail rate. Now let's assume we determine that 20 percent of these bookings are incremental (some analytics approaches to determine this are covered later in this chapter). Graphically, it looks like Figure 6.2.

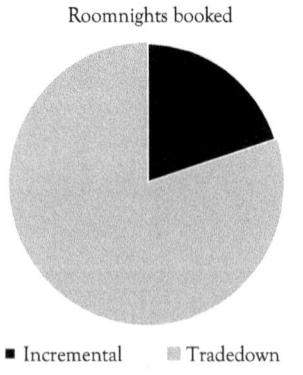

Figure 6.2 Roomnights—Incremental vs Tradedown

Well, we have booked plenty of incremental RN, so this should make us happy, right? Not so fast. How much of the *revenue* is incremental? We booked 1,000 RN at $105 (the 30 percent discount), or $105,000. Without the discount, we would have booked 800 RN at $150, or $120,000! This is a money loser, because the discount is larger than the incremental percentage. If the incremental percentage had been 30 percent, or if the discount had been 20 percent, the revenues would be the same with or without this discounted rate. That said, the assessment of any such discounted rate also needs to take costs into account. Generating the same revenue on more RN will have a negative profit impact, because each incremental roomnight has some associated cost, such as housekeeping and utilities (for the moment, we are ignoring any incremental ancillary spend).

Let's look at a different example. Consider the college professor discount of 30 percent. But now, let's assume that 50 percent of the RN are incremental. How much of the revenue is incremental? With the discount, we booked 1,000 RN at $105, for a total revenue of $105,000. Without the discount, we would have booked 500 RN (the 50 percent that are tradedown), at a rate of $150, for a total revenue of $75,000. So, $30k of the $105k booked was incremental. Another way to think about this is that 29 percent of the revenue is incremental. An important takeaway here is that when you are measuring *incremental percent*, that slice of the pie gets smaller (less positive or more negative) when you move from RN to revenue. Figures 6.3 and 6.4 illustrate this with the example we just discussed.

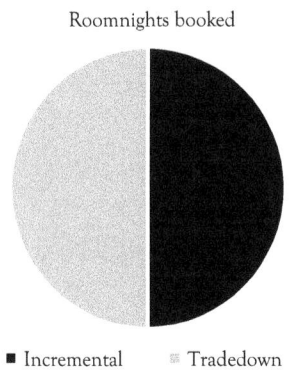

Figure 6.3 Roomnights—Incremental vs Tradedown

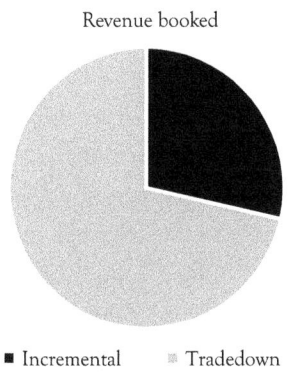

Figure 6.4 Revenue—Incremental vs Tradedown

Additionally, the incremental benefit may get smaller still when you move from revenue to profit, as each of these incremental RN has some associated cost, as noted earlier (caveat: there may, however, be additional revenues from nonroom spending that need to be taken into account). Based on the preceding example, the resulting pie chart, accounting for incremental costs, may look something like Figure 6.5.

"Profit" booked

■ Incremental   ■ Incr. Cost   ■ Tradedown

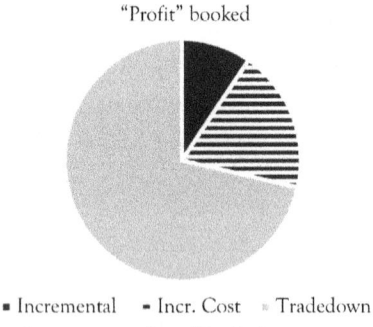

Figure 6.5 Profit—Incremental vs Tradedown

Well, it is clear that in order for any discounted rate to add value, it needs to be highly incremental, meaning notably in excess of the discount percentage. How can we drive the incremental percentage? The most important way is to target a more price-sensitive audience (see Condition #2). Another way is to promote it. With no promotion, the only people who know of this discount are people who are already looking to book with you and happen to see it, which of course is a guarantee of significant tradedown.

One common fallacy related to discounted rates is worth noting here. You may hear something like "we can make this fully *yieldable*, and the hotel will only take this business when it wants/needs it," which implies that there is only upside. This is *not at all* true. *Yieldable does not mean incremental!* The previous statement is worth committing to memory, as it is so often misunderstood. Making a given discount rate yieldable is generally beneficial to the hotel, whether that discount rate is a money loser or not. But making a money losing discount rate yieldable is like saying "I have a bad idea, but I'll only do it part of the time to limit the damage." A money losing discount rate that is yieldable is still a money loser! Bob Cross, Chairman of Revenue Analytics, says that the worst practices in pricing all come under the heading of *undisciplined discounting*. He emphasizes that "broad-based, carpet-bombing discounts are an indiscriminate way to grow volume, and they invariably lead to collateral damage." Wise words indeed.

When considering discounted rates, such as promotional rates, another important variable is the size of the audience. As a very general rule, there is a tradeoff between size and incremental percentage. I could design a discount program that is close to 100 percent incremental, but brings in only five bookings; this would be a lot of effort for not much benefit. The larger my target audience, the more the risk of tradedown (again, this is a generalization). For example, at a discount of 20 percent, I'd rather have 1,000 bookings with 40 percent incrementality than five bookings at 100 percent incrementality.

Price Discrimination and Screening

The term *price discrimination* may have a negative connotation to some, but it has a positive connotation to me, because it means charging different people different prices based on their price sensitivity, and making money in the process ☺. One obvious example is seen in movie theaters (pre-COVID, and hopefully post-COVID as well); they charge a lower price for the young and the old, and more to those in between, based on price sensitivity, in this case driven by differences in disposable income.

Earlier in this chapter, we saw the two criteria for a discounted rate. The example we have been using is a *qualified rate* (you have to be a college professor, with the appropriate ID). Now let's consider a *fenced* rate (meaning you have to do something to earn it). One important factor in a customer's price sensitivity is this: Am I paying with my own money or someone else's money? A proxy for this may be: Am I traveling for leisure or business? I may want to charge less if the customer is traveling on vacation (and paying for it themselves), as this customer may be more price-sensitive than a customer traveling on business. How would I know the purpose of their trip? I can't really ask the customer, "are you traveling for leisure or business?" or "are you paying for this yourself?" or "how price sensitive are you?" As an aside, some sites do ask about trip purpose, but it is usually after the booking is made, and therefore not an input into pricing. Is there some way to determine how price-sensitive a customer is? I should point out here for clarity that price sensitivity doesn't necessarily apply to a person over time; rather, it applies to a person on a specific occasion. A customer may be highly price-sensitive on one trip, and relatively price-insensitive on the next; actually this is quite common.

Airlines figured price discrimination out early. Consider a roundtrip flight from Washington DC to Chicago. For example, let's assume that business travelers (paying with company money) will pay $1,000, but leisure customers (paying with their own money) will pay no more than $400. The airline would really like to get those willing to pay $1,000 to actually pay $1,000, but also get some additional customers who will pay only $400. The airline wants to know whether the customer is on leisure or business travel, to assess their price sensitivity, and therefore the price they should be charged. But they can't ask that. So ... they *ask* "are you willing?" to stay over a Saturday night (of course, they don't really ask this question—they use booking rules to ask and answer it). Customers who stay over a Saturday are far less likely to be traveling on business. And a business traveler is unlikely to extend their stay to save their company some money. So, a customer will be charged $1,000 unless they are staying over a Saturday night, in which case they'll be charged $400. Clever, huh? For readers familiar with the field of the game theory, this is called *screening*. Screening means setting up a situation where (in this case) the customer has to make a decision, and this decision *reveals* something useful about that customer. This is a critical element of price discrimination.

Once such decision that may provide some useful information is when a booking involves a nonrefundable advance-purchase rate. By accepting such a rate, the customer has just revealed that they are willing to lock in a booking, and are unlikely to change it. To the extent that this behavior is more typical of leisure travelers, we have identified a price discrimination opportunity. In practice, results from advance-purchase rates are mixed, though on balance positive, based on assessments of the experts I interviewed for this book. Why are they not more incremental? One reason is that some hotel operators may not have put much thought into the appropriate booking window or discount level (this is a broad statement, with notable exceptions). For example, should my hotel's advance-purchase rate be 10 percent off if you book a week out, or 30 percent off if you book three weeks out? The latter is likely to be more incremental (of course depending on the business versus leisure booking windows at the given hotel), but smaller in volume. Another reason advance-purchase rates are not more incremental is because of the growth of last-minute deals. Price-sensitive customers may want to wait for a discount, as opposed to lock in an advance-purchase booking to get a discount. What's a hotel to do?

With the huge caveat that this is quite dependent on other decisions of the hotel and the competitor hotels, as well as customer expectations ... here are a few thoughts: Don't offer last-minute rates if you can avoid it (and for the love of all that you hold dear, don't offer them exclusively on third-party channels, if you hope to have any sense of channel control). Offering last-minute deals *trains* your customers to wait until the last minute to book, which by necessity puts downward pressure on your retail rates. Decisions on advance-purchase rates should be driven by the market. By this, I mean that you should not be the only hotel among your competitors to offer an advance-purchase rate. If it doesn't work, meaning, it doesn't drive sufficient incremental volume to offset the discount, you'll lose money. And if it works, your competition will notice, and you'll trigger a price war for that portion of your booking window. Either way, you lose. On the other hand, if advance-purchase rates are common in your market, you should probably offer them as well, of course yielding them in peak times. The reason for this is that if your hotel is the only one without an advance-purchase rate, and assuming you are priced properly at the retail rate, you will effectively be overpriced for that *advance* portion of your booking window.

One screening technique that has yet to be implemented in hospitality: day/time of booking. If my hotel has several bookings for a one-night stay next Wednesday, how can I tell which are more likely to be for leisure travel? It turns out that the great majority of business bookings are made during business hours (some small number of exceptions). If a booking is made at 9 pm during the week, or on a Saturday, it is much more likely to be a leisure booking. As an illustrative example, my retail price for Wednesday of next week may be $200; when I leave work on Friday, I could change that to $175, then Monday morning change it back to $200. In this way, I have lowered my price for those customers who are likely to be staying on leisure (note that this screening technique is based on the day of week the booking was *made*, rather than the arrival/departure dates). There are of course some practical considerations to actually using this information for pricing, such as any price shopping software or services, and the corresponding cancelation window, which could impact the likelihood of a cancel/rebook. That said, I encourage the reader to use this example to understand the concept of screening for purposes of price discrimination and also to consider how you might implement this.

Opaque Rates

What about opaque rates? Before we leave this chapter on discount rates, I want to cover one clear example of a fenced discount rate that *can* (italics are important here) be highly incremental: opaque rates. Chris Anderson, Professor at Cornell, points out that opaque models have evolved over time, and now provide hotels more help with last-minute bookings; he emphasized "the whole idea is to break out price sensitive customers." Recall the preceding discussion about screening. One way for the customer to make a decision that reveals information about their price sensitivity: agree to book a hotel without knowing which hotel it is! They could pay a bit more to pick exactly which hotel they want, but they have chosen not to. That said, there is one critical element of the opaque model that, in my view, does not get nearly enough attention: the *size* of the *neighborhoods*. When a customer books through an opaque channel, they select a neighborhood and a star level, and sometimes other features too. But a really small neighborhood does not require the customer to risk much. To illustrate this point, consider two different downtown neighborhoods, one with a radius of five blocks, and one with a radius of 5 miles. In the latter, a customer willing to book an unknown hotel and willing to travel a long distance has demonstrated a high price sensitivity; this is not true for the former. To make this real, consider the Washington DC market. For a particular trip, let's assume that the customer really wants to be near the convention center, but the nearby hotels of the desired star level are all charging high rates. An opaque model that guarantees that the customer will be within a few *blocks* doesn't really separate out the price-sensitive customers. Alternatively, an opaque model that will put the customer somewhere within a few *miles* will certainly identify those price-sensitive customers. My advice to hotels and hotel companies: push for larger neighborhoods from these opaque channels. In my opinion, this is *more important* than any controls on bidding rules, preference, margin, volume limits, ... and even more important than the discount level itself! You will get pushback of course: "but a large neighborhood is customer-unfriendly." Yes, but in this case, it is this screening technique that segments out the truly price-sensitive customers to reduce tradedown, and therefore is *precisely* why it is hotel-friendly!

Measuring Success

So far in this chapter, we've been discussing the requirement that discounted rates drive sufficient incremental volume, not just overall volume. In the remainder of this chapter, let's cover some specific techniques that can be used to evaluate the incrementality percentage of an existing discount rate, and thereby determine if this discount rate should be continued, changed, or eliminated. We'll review A/B testing, repeat behavior analysis, and pattern analysis, and apply them to the evaluation of discount rates. Then I'll add a few words of caution related to promotional rates and distribution channels.

After a discount rate is in place, how would you know if it is working? By *working*, I mean generating incremental revenue, and not simply recording bookings, as described earlier. And if there is meaningful marginal cost, we want to measure incremental profit. Here, I'll focus on how to measure the incrementality of roomnight volume. From there, the calculation of incremental revenue is quite straightforward, following the college professor example shown earlier. There are a few ways to measure the effect of a discounted rate. Which approach is best depends on issues such as the following:

- Is the discount relatively new or has it been in place for a long time?
- Are you able to evaluate performance of multiple hotels, or do you just have access to a single hotel's data?
- Is the discount available at all of your hotels?
- Is the discount yieldable?

Let's talk through some approaches.

A/B Testing

To state the obvious, this is only applicable if you have an A and a B. If you are evaluating a specific discount program that is in place at some hotels, and not in place at other similar hotels, this approach can work. If you are just looking at a single hotel, and you have valid A and B timeframes (before and after, for example), this A/B approach may work. Important note: the smaller the data set (e.g., fewer hotels, less time, fewer bookings), the more the risk of statistical insignificance. I won't get into significance tests in this book, as plenty has been written about it; with a Google search on *significance testing*, you will have over 200M articles to pick from. In short, if a test produces results that are not *statistically significant*, at a specified level of confidence, this means that the results may be due to a random effect rather than the measured effect. Skepticism is in order—true in general when interpreting such results. It is also possible that random effects mask a real effect, meaning that the discount rate is actually working, but the results don't support that conclusion. To paraphrase the British physicist Martin Rees, absence of evidence is not evidence of absence.

A word of caution on A/B tests to measure incrementality: If the discount rate is yieldable, the A/B results are easy to misinterpret. I've seen this first-hand. Let's consider the college professor rate noted previously. Let's say we do some A/B testing and determine that days with bookings of this rate underperform days without, and also that hotels that book a lot of this rate underperform hotels that book little of it. Let's assume that both measurements are statistically significant. This discounted rate clearly didn't work, case closed, right? …. Not quite. Because this rate is yieldable, and because revenue managers presumably only make it available on lower demand days (because of the deep discount), the measured A/B results are actually reflective of the demand environment rather than the impact of the rate itself; you'll only see this rate booked when demand is weak. In this case, this is not a valid A/B test because the days this rate is offered and the hotels offering these rates are *not* similar between A and B.

In reality, A/B testing is a starting point to more detailed analysis. I refer the reader to an excellent article, *A/B Testing is the Tricycle of Analytics*, by Mike Lukianoff, whom I had the pleasure of speaking with when I started this book. In the article, Mike makes the point that A/B testing is great in situations where there is a *clean* A and B, but it falls short in many other cases where there are multiple variables, hence the need for so-called *multivariate testing*. For the purposes of measuring incrementality of discount rates, which is the focus of this chapter, I recommend beginning with A/B testing; if you find that there is not an obvious A and B, or if there are other variables that could impact results, such as price variations or different marketing efforts at different times, then you may need to *upgrade* your analysis to multivariate testing.

Another way to think about A/B testing is that it can work well in a binary environment. This means that the effect you're trying to isolate is a single variable that is either *on* or *off*; for example, a given hotel either did or did not participate in a specified promotion, or a hotel did or did not install a new system, or a consumer was or was not exposed to certain digital content.

Repeat Behavior

Another way to measure the effectiveness of a given discount rate is to look at repeat behavior of individual guests. Let's keep using the college professor rate as an example. Let's further assume that I have the ability to track individual guests, across multiple devices, or that I have the ability to make some adjustments if such tracking is imperfect. If I look at the 1,000 bookings at this rate, I can determine how many different people that is. Let's assume there are 500 professors who have booked this rate. Now I want to determine if I have seen these people before, and if so, at what rate? Note that tracking past behavior can be at the same hotel where the professor booked this discount rate, in the same market, same region, or considering all hotels for which I have data. These different cuts will provide different results, and those results mean different things, details of which are as follows.

To continue the example, of the 500 professors who booked this rate at a given hotel, and looking at their booking behavior in the past year, let's assume I have seen 25 of them at this same hotel, 100 of them in the same market, and 200 of them in any hotel (for which I have data). If those are the repeat rates that I measure, what does this all mean? Well, not much just yet. I've seen 200 of them before, but it would be wrong to interpret that to mean that this discount rate brought in 300 new customers. Why? Because there is a lot of *churn* in the hotel business. We see a lot of new customers, and a lot of customers who don't come back. So, I'll want to compare the repeat behavior of these professors (the *test set*) to the repeat behavior of those people booking the retail rate (the *control set*). Now I must construct a control set of people who booked retail rate at the selected hotel during the same time frame. It is critical that these people be *matched* as closely as possible to the professors who booked, in terms of frequency of stays, loyalty level, average length of stay, and other parameters (the better the matching, the more *pure* the measured effect). The reason this matching is so critical is that if the matching is only *pretty good*, you can get skewed results. For example, consider the college professor bookings; you are likely to measure that the test set of college professors has a much lower repeat rate than the control set of overall retail customers. But the main driver of this is that college professors travel less frequently than the average retail customer, many of whom are frequent business travelers. So, you may interpret the results to mean that this rate is highly incremental, when in fact it just shows that you didn't set up your control set very well.

Now let's assume that I find 5,000 such matches. This means that I find 5,000 people with a similar profile in terms of loyalty, frequency, and so on, similar in every way except that they are not professors, and therefore, they don't book the professor rate. Note that this matching is at the individual guest level, as opposed to matching parameters for the group. Now let's assume I determine that I've seen 500 of these people at the selected hotel in the past year (and they paid retail then too). So, I have professors with a repeat rate of 5 percent at this hotel (25/500) and a control set with a repeat rate of 10 percent (500/5000). What does this mean? It means that I can infer that this discount program is 50 percent incremental! How? If it were 100 percent incremental, the professor repeat rate would be 0 percent. If it were 0 percent incremental, the repeat rate would mirror the overall repeat rate of 10 percent. For any math nerds reading, the resulting formula is:

Incrementality percent = 1 − (professor repeat rate/matched-people repeat rate).

Note that this incrementality measure can be evaluated for the market as well. Let's assume that the market repeat rate for the professors, and the matched set (of the 500 professors, or of the 5,000 matched guests, how many have I seen in the same market in the past year) is 6 and 11 percent, respectively. Using the same formula, this means that this discount rate is 45.5 percent incremental to the market. In this example, the fact that the hotel incrementality is greater than the market incrementality means that some hotels can steal professor bookings from other hotels. The same approach holds true for incrementality to a brand, to a tier, to a country, globally, and so on. The reason to consider incrementality in these different contexts is that it is often the case that a given discount is incremental to the hotel, but not to a larger set of hotels; for example, a discount at an upper upscale hotel may just be stealing business from a nearby upscale hotel in the same portfolio of brands. Whether this is good or not depends on one's perspective. To add to the complexity a bit, the professors and the matched set have likely booked a variety of rate types in the past. This can be accounted for by using the appropriate discount percentage in the calculations of how much revenue is incremental. For example, if the professors used to all book some other rate at 10 percent off retail, then the discount is effectively 20 percent (30 percent off retail versus 10 percent off retail) for the purposes of calculating the incremental revenue.

Just for fun, here is a picture from one of my notebooks—this one from 2010. We were testing a *Florida Resident Rate*. The idea was that perhaps local residents were more price-sensitive than people who were traveling long distances to come to Florida. It turns out that this was not true, as my poorly written notes in Figure 6.6 indicate. At the risk of stating the obvious, I'm not saying that the test was a bad idea. Many people, myself included, thought this had a decent chance of success, and we would not have known otherwise had we not tested it.

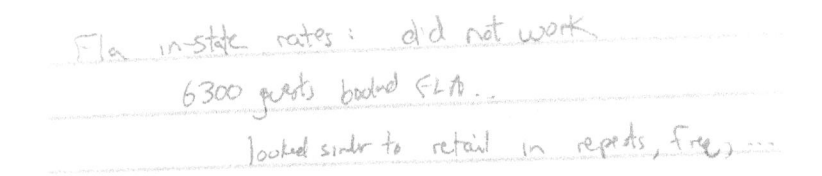

Figure 6.6 Notes—In-State rates

Mix Versus Yield

If a given discount has been in place for a while, say several years, then the repeat behavior may not be very instructive, meaning you won't see *new* customers because of this rate. And if it is widely available across hotels, A/B testing may prove untenable as it will be difficult to construct a valid A and B. However, if this rate is yieldable, there is another approach available. For simplicity, let's assume that college professors only book either the retail rate or the professor rate. If I look at all of the bookings of professors, some percentage will be the professor rate and some will be retail. I can compare this to the percentage of time that the professor rate is available (weighted by the usage at each hotel). For example, if the professor rate is available 50 percent of the time, and of all professors' bookings, 50 percent are at the professor rate and 50 percent are at retail, I can infer that none of the professor bookings is incremental. How? You'd see this result if every professor decided to book a given hotel, and then looked to see if the professor rate was open (if yes, book it; if no, book retail). By definition, this means it is not bringing in new customers. If, however, we see that 100 percent of professors' bookings are at the professor rate, despite only being available 50 percent of the time, this means that this rate is 100 percent incremental (they will only book this rate; there is no tradedown). If 75 percent of professors' bookings are at the professor rate, and it is available 50 percent of the time, you can infer that 50 percent of the bookings are incremental. Again, for the math nerds, the formula I'm using is:

Incrementality percent = (mix percent − availability percent)/(1 − availability percent).

As one more example, using this formula, if a given rate is available 25 percent of the time, and it is booked 40 percent of the time by a given set of customers, we can infer that this rate is 20 percent incremental, and it better have a discount shallower than 20 percent to generate incremental revenue. What if the mix percentage is less than the availability percentage? This means that people don't even book it when it is open, implying a lack of awareness, so the incrementality would be dreadful, but at least the magnitude would be limited ☹/☺.

Before we close this chapter, two points of caution are in order. The first point of caution is that there are two main components to a discount rate program, the discount itself and the marketing behind it, and the evaluation must reflect that. If a given promotion does not generate incremental revenue, it may be because it was not promoted aggressively enough, or it may be that the offer was not compelling enough, or some combination. In my experience, it is far too common to assign the combined effect to only one of these components.

The second point of caution has to do with distribution channels, specifically discounted rates on these channels. It is quite possible to put a discounted rate on a third-party channel, and then measure that it is highly incremental (in this example, likely driven by preferential display). This means that the customers booking on that channel are customers you haven't seen before (or haven't tracked). This of course invites the question: can I put retail rates on this site? If your hotel is required to put discounts on this site, you may still measure a high level of incrementality, even for revenue. *But ...* as customers learn about this, and they will, they will begin defecting from your direct channels. This is the exact opposite of a sound distribution strategy ☹. Another way to think about this example: channel incrementality declines over time.

The broad misunderstanding of discounted rates applies well beyond hospitality. I refer the reader to an excellent white paper on the topic by Bain & Company, entitled *Bringing Order to Discounts Gone Haywire*, from May 2020. In the article, the authors note that in many cases, discounts "have not been subject to the kind of scrutiny that management gives to more explicit costs." That comment is worth memorizing.

In conclusion for this chapter, let me emphasize that making decisions that drive incremental revenue, and ultimately incremental profit over time, is at the heart of revenue strategy. This concept applies across segments, and across channels, and requires some tradeoffs. These tradeoffs can be short term versus long term, acquisition versus retention, customer engagement versus profit, and so on. More broadly, these tradeoffs reflect decisions on planning and resource allocation, which as Cindy Estis Green, CEO and Cofounder of Kalibri Labs, notes, is the essence of strategy.

CHAPTER 7

Negotiated Account Rates

A Look at Last Room Availability, Qualification, and Dynamic Pricing

The topic of this chapter could be an entire book by itself. And the topic is especially relevant to the recovery phase of an economic cycle. Negotiated account rates are those rates that are agreed to by an account and a specific hotel, for a specified timeframe. For example, Company X can stay at Hotel Y during a given calendar year for $149. I'm oversimplifying here; sometimes these rates vary seasonally, sometimes they apply to more than one hotel, sometimes the rates are a percent discount off retail as opposed to a fixed rate, and sometimes there are other parameters involved such as value-adds or less restrictive cancel policies. Negotiated account rates typically lag in a recovery, with a dampening effect on ADR, often for years. The COVID-19 pandemic has caused the most significant downturn in demand in history, and the industry's fortunes are in large part dependent on how well we navigate the recovery in this segment. There are of course *many* aspects to account pricing that are beyond the scope of this book; perhaps these are topics I'll pursue for my next book ☺. In this chapter, I want to cover three aspects of negotiated account rates in particular: (a) last room availability (LRA, referring to a hotel's ability to control inventory), (b) *cheaters*, referring to guests who book a rate for which they do not qualify, and (c) dynamic pricing (in a negotiated rate context). And please note that a related topic, price *modeling* for negotiated accounts, is covered in detail in Chapter 5.

Last Room Availability

LRA has been a pain point for hoteliers for many years. As a brief reminder, LRA means that if a hotel has a standard room to sell at retail rate, it must make that room available to any negotiated account with

LRA in their contract (which is the overwhelming majority of accounts). Accounts certainly like this feature, but hotels would prefer that accounts not have it. Some grounding: accounts negotiate discounted rates with a hotel (for large hotel companies, the process is a bit more involved), and these discounts can range from 5 percent to 40 percent or more. In return for these (often) deep discounts, the account pushes volume to a selected hotel. The hotel operator needs to decide on the value of this business by considering the revenue the account brings and weighing that against the days when the hotel could sell those rooms for a higher rate (displacement is discussed in Chapter 2), and of course how much of that account business the hotel could get at the retail rate (tradedown is also discussed in Chapter 2). A good revenue manager would know the dates when the hotel can sell higher rates and close out these lower negotiated rates. But ... accounts/travel managers know this, and they want availability, even (especially) in high demand times, and so they include *LRA* in their contracts. In effect, this means that the hotel cannot close the account rate unless they also close every other rate including retail. We, as an industry, have talked about how this impacts our hotels' ability to drive rate and what we could do about it. Many in the industry, from large chains to small independents to franchise operators to owners, have talked about negotiating LRA out of these contracts, with extremely little success. As an aside, some hotels *play games* with room definitions; because LRA typically only applies to standard rooms, a hotel can add some small amenity to a standard room, designate it a *premium,* and make it unavailable to lower priced accounts. For the record, I do *not* recommend this, as I believe it is unethical. So, what to do? One approach is to look at the guaranteed availability as an option. By this, I do not mean a *choice*, I mean look at it like a financial option—for example, a stock option. A hotel that has an account with LRA has effectively sold a *call option* on that capacity. The account now owns the call option. Just like with a stock option, the owner of a call option has the right but not the obligation to purchase the underlying asset at a predetermined price—in this case, the negotiated rate. Note that, absent any volume guarantees from the account, which are rare, all of the risk is borne by the hotel. The account is under no obligation, and in fact, if another hotel later undercuts the given hotel's price by enough, the account can switch all of their business. My point here is not that a hotel should get in the business of selling options. My point is that if a hotel is giving up guaranteed availability (as opposed to providing a yieldable rate), that has a value that should be reflected in the rate. I highly recommend that hotel operators, and revenue managers in particular, price accounts in this context. For example, a hotel could offer an account one of two rates, one with LRA or one without (but not both). The price differential would be determined by the option value of the LRA, and this would vary greatly by hotel, and perhaps even by account for a given hotel. For example, LRA at a high demand hotel has more value than at a low demand hotel. Furthermore, accounts with stay patterns that overindex on peak nights will derive more option value from LRA. Hotels with significant fluctuations in demand will also be giving up more value with LRA; for example, an account could stay at the selected hotel on peak nights when the retail rates are much higher than the negotiated rate, but stay at a competitor hotel on low demand nights when a competitor retail rate might drop below the given hotel's negotiated rate. In this case, eliminating the account's *call option* would be beneficial to the hotel.

So, how would we calculate this option value? A little grounding in probability is called for. Option valuation is based on probabilities. Readers with a finance bent will know that the Black–Scholes option pricing formula is based on probabilities. If there were no probability involved, then the value of LRA would be a very straightforward calculation (negotiated rate minus displacement value each day). What might it look like with probability involved? Let's consider a single week at a *typical* hotel. We expect Sundays to be low demand; Mondays, Thursdays, and Fridays to be moderate demand; and Tuesdays, Wednesdays, and Saturdays to be high demand. But we don't know exactly what will happen on a given day, hence the probabilities. There are many different *flavors* of displacement models. At its most simplistic, a displacement model will consider a booking (or potential booking), look at other available demand, and return some measure of the revenue displaced. Such models are fairly easy to build with only basic functions in Excel and a bit of history. Let's assume we have such a displacement model that returns the percentage of the negotiated account rate that is displaced. This percentage could range from 0 percent (no displacement) to some figure above 100 percent (meaning it displaces a higher rated booking). Using a simulation, with some estimates of demand by day of week, could produce results like those in Figure 7.1.

Day	Dislp%1	Dislp%2	Dislp%3	Dislp%4	Dislp%5	AVG
SUN	0%	4%	9%	14%	4%	6%
MON	32%	45%	51%	34%	24%	37%
TUE	96%	65%	71%	64%	68%	73%
WED	53%	48%	78%	71%	64%	63%
THU	27%	11%	31%	20%	24%	23%
FRI	55%	41%	39%	28%	57%	44%
SAT	105%	80%	91%	81%	65%	85%

Figure 7.1 Example of displacement simulation

What does this mean? In this simple example, there are 5 simulations (Displ%1–Displ%5); each simulation has the exact same inputs, except for a random number generator that is used to estimate the actual demand, based on an expected distribution, upon which the displacement is calculated. Each simulation generates a displacement estimate for each day of week, as shown. The AVG column at the end is the average of the 5 simulations. For example, we see that for this particular account at this hotel for this week, we expect that on Monday, any account RN will displace 37 percent of their revenue (see the AVG column for MON). This means that for every $100 of account revenue, we expect to displace $37 on that particular day. This type of table is fairly easy to replicate for every day of the year and across multiple hotels. The important point is that it is used to determine the expected value of LRA, and *price* that option accordingly.

One more point on LRA: Even though LRA accounts are not yieldable (by definition), their existence may influence your overall yielding strategy, in an interesting, and perhaps counterintuitive, way. Consider a hotel where most of the negotiated business books three weeks out, and most of the retail business books two weeks out. Now assume you are looking at a peak demand night in the future. At three weeks out, you could close the retail and negotiated segments, essentially closing everything, except possibly some loyalty redemptions. Why would you do this? If you are expecting a sellout, and you'd like to leave availability for high-priced retail business, you would stop selling during the portion of the booking window when most of the bookings will be discounted rates, and reopen when most of the bookings will be retail. Some hotels do this today, with varying levels of *aggression*.

Cheaters

The second topic I want to address in this negotiated account rates chapter is *cheaters*. Hotels put a lot of time and effort into determining an appropriate negotiated account rate, with the expectation that the travel manager has some significant degree of control over where his/her associates stay. BUT ... sometimes, someone who does not qualify for that discounted rate will book it. For example, if XYZ Corp has a negotiated rate at the Valley Inn hotel, it is not difficult for another customer to figure out how to book that rate, when they really should be booking the higher retail rate. Such a booking is a direct revenue hit to the hotel, even though *some* of it may be incremental. It is not practical, in most cases, to ask for ID at the desk, as this can put the front desk associates in an awkward position (e.g., how would they know if XYZ Corp has several subsidiaries with different names?). A technology solution is called for, the details of which (including the strictness and associated tradeoffs) will need to be determined by each hotel company. To make this case, meaning the business case to warrant a significant technology investment to address the cheater issue, we'd need to know the magnitude of the problem. The *cheater %*, meaning the percentage of bookings at negotiated rates that are not qualified for that rate, ranges from 5 percent to well over 25 percent, depending on whom you speak with (and I've spoken with several people from several different companies). Can we measure this? Probably not directly, because for any given booking, it is difficult to determine actual qualification. But we can estimate it, or more precisely, we can put a lower bound on it. Here's how: track every booking at every negotiated rate, by customer. Each booking will have an associated company or organization. Both the tracking by customer, as well as the assignment of a rate to a specific account, takes some work. But it can be done. Then, look at the number of account-specific rates booked by each customer. For example, see the table in Figure 7.2.

64 HOTEL REVENUE MANAGEMENT

Matthew Hughes	Bookings	% of Total
XYZ Corp	8	42%
ABC Corp	5	26%
Tech_Int Corp	3	16%
HHL P Firm	3	16%

Figure 7.2 Frequency of account-specific rates

This particular guest, Matthew Hughes, had 19 different bookings, across a given portfolio, at negotiated rates. Of course, we would want to track customers by more than just their first and last name (loyalty #, company, address, phone #, etc.). We could take a conservative approach, and give Mr. Hughes the benefit of the doubt, and assume that the account with the largest number of bookings is *legit*. In this case, that would mean that Mr. Hughes *cheats* 58 percent of the time, meaning that 58 percent of his bookings at an account rate are associated with a company for which he does not work. Some caveats are warranted. Clearly, this type of analysis is much easier with a large sample of hotels. Depending on the time frame investigated, we may need to make some adjustments for job changers; perhaps two of the accounts are legit, though the sequence of the bookings will matter in this determination. The analyst doing this work will also want to account for the total number of bookings (fewer total bookings mean that concentration in a single account is more likely); the preceding generous assumption may significantly underestimate the cheater percentage. Takeaway: if your organization has more than a handful of hotels, this *cheater analysis* could be revealing, and could help justify a business case to address it.

Dynamic Pricing

To close out this chapter on negotiated account rates, I want to briefly cover a concept called *dynamic pricing*. The term *dynamic pricing* has many definitions. In the context of negotiated rates, it means rates that float as a percentage discount off retail. Hotels like the concept of dynamic pricing, as this allows for account rates to increase if demand (and therefore retail rates) warrants. Accounts also like, and push for, *dynamic pricing*. Well, if hotels and accounts *both* like dynamic pricing, why is it so rare? The answer is that hotels and accounts mean slightly different things. Consider a large account and a large hotel chain. Even the largest account only has negotiated rates at a small percentage of the chain's hotels, those where they have meaningful volume. Everywhere else, employees of that account pay retail, or some other rate such as advance-purchase. Hotels would like to take those negotiated rates and make them *floating* as opposed to *fixed*. But when accounts speak of dynamic pricing, their desire is to keep the high-volume hotels at fixed rates, *and* then have a floating discount everywhere else (meaning they never pay retail)! Some high value accounts already have just such an arrangement with some of the large chains. All that said, I believe it is worthwhile for hotels (and of course large hotel chains) to pursue dynamic pricing at high volume hotels. A fixed negotiated rate has inherent risk to the hotel. If demand falls in a market, hotels are likely to renegotiate their fixed rates down, or else risk losing the volume to a lower-priced competitor. But if the market demand grows, the hotel is stuck with the low fixed rate. With fixed rates, to recap: if demand increases, the hotel loses; if demand decreases, the hotel does *not* win. As an aside, I teach this theme in my classes: don't take a risk unless you get paid for it (this theme applies broadly to business in general). Fixed account rates are another example of an *option*, also similar to a financial option. The account has the right, but not the obligation, to purchase those rooms at a fixed price. Moving to dynamic pricing can shift some of this risk from the hotel to the account, and hotel companies should properly value this risk reduction, similar to the preceding discussion on valuing LRA as an option. Another risk mitigation approach is of course volume guarantees, where the given parameters of price and LRA are predicated on volume targets from the account. I believe this will be a growing, and very welcome, factor in account pricing. This would entail regular, perhaps quarterly, *account reviews* with each significant account; if production is meaningfully below expectations, then the hotel would have the option (meaning the right but not the obligation) to adjust parameters such as pricing or LRA.

As you can see from our discussion in this chapter, there is a lot of complexity to account pricing, and we've only scratched the surface.

Based on my numerous interviews for this book, this is a critically important segment of business, and we as an industry are merely *OK* at this. To advance as a discipline, we need to get better at this. As we evolve to revenue strategy, we need to be very good at this, with supporting goals and analytics, and in the larger context of how we spend our time and money.

CHAPTER 8

Distribution and Loyalty

Tactical and Strategic Implications for Revenue Management

In Chapter 2, we discussed how revenue management can be thought of as maximizing the *benefit* to hotels, which is a bit different than maximizing hotel-level profitability. In this chapter, I'd like to unpack that concept, with a focus on distribution and loyalty. It is beyond the scope of this book to do a deep dive into either distribution or loyalty, as each could fill a book on their own (now added to my to-do list ☺). Rather, my intention is to connect the dots to revenue management's evolution to revenue strategy.

Loyalty and distribution decisions will influence, and be influenced by, pricing and inventory decisions. For example, a hotel or set of hotels may choose to offer *member rates* (also called *loyalty rates*) on direct channels. Many hotels also offer some form of promotional *member offers,* also usually on direct channels. A note on terminology: I use the term *member rates* to mean the rates that are available to members at a very shallow discount off retail; I use the term *member offers* to mean more deeply discounted rates that are available to members but are only used on a promotional basis. From a *tactical* standpoint, both of these are likely bad ideas. Why? They result in tradedown. One of the two criteria for a (successful) discount rate is that the rate is targeted to an audience that is more price sensitive than the overall retail segment. It would be very difficult to make that case for loyalty members; in fact, they tend to be less price-sensitive. So, a discount would be an unwise tactic here. Specifically, a hotel is likely to bring in *less* revenue with such *member rates* and *member offers.* But this chapter is more about strategy than tactics. A discounted loyalty rate, as a part of a more holistic package of enticing benefits, may make the loyalty program itself more appealing, and therefore drive membership, and this has tremendous benefits to the hotel and to the brand and portfolio.

Loyalty is a clear driver of consumer decisions, and plenty of research backs this up. Loyalty also impacts price sensitivity; the more engaged a customer is with a brand or a portfolio of brands, the less sensitive they will be to price. It also impacts channel choice, as more engaged customers tend to overindex on direct channels. If you, as a hotelier, can influence customer behavior and drive engagement such that the customer searches for lodging options on your website or app, and only considers your brand or portfolio (or even your particular hotel), you have accomplished something of great value. In this context, a bit of a loss leader in pricing can be a wise approach.

That said, there is a really important nuance at play here, one that resonated with many of the industry leaders I interviewed for this book. If a hotel or set of hotels offers a discounted rate to loyalty members for the purposes of stimulating demand in a need time, that is, *member offers*, this is likely to actually reduce revenue during that need time. It doesn't require a great deal of high-level revenue strategy thinking to determine that if you are approaching a low revenue time, it is unwise to implement something that will reduce your revenues ☹. Based on my research for this book, this is an exceedingly common mistake. Rather, discounted rates to members should be targeted to specific members who are likely to increase their engagement because of a particular offer. And in many cases, these targeted offers should be points-based rather than price-based, the former often being more likely to drive engagement. Matt Busch, Senior Vice President at Equifax, describes a common and significant error in approach to member offers: assuming loyalty members are the same in terms of engagement. Matt puts a fine point on it, "the vast majority, likely above 80 percent, of loyalty members are only slightly more engaged with a brand or portfolio than those on an externally purchased mailing list." The revenue strategist of the future needs to view a loyalty program as a way to drive customer behavior. Broadly speaking, a loyalty program should be focused on *influencing* behavior, rather than merely recognizing behavior. Though these are related, they are most certainly not the same.

It would be difficult to argue that customers, especially loyalty members, booking on a direct channel tend to be more price-sensitive than similar customers booking on a third-party channel, and that therefore we should have preferential pricing on direct channels. But if we believe (and I do) that preferential channel pricing can, also as part of a holistic set of loyalty and channel benefits, actually influence a customer's choice of channel, then this can be a wise pricing strategy, especially given the different costs of bookings from different channels. And of course, driving engagement with direct channels also involves driving engagement with the loyalty program—these should be thought of as inextricably linked.

Astute readers will note that this loyalty and channel dynamic applies beyond just pricing; there may be inventory considerations as well. Many brand companies offer preferential availability to high-level loyalty members, essentially allowing them to make some bookings that would otherwise be restricted—for example, allowing an elite loyalty member to book an unappealing (to the hotel) stay pattern. In addition, a hotel may, and several do, yield third-party channels more aggressively than they do direct channels with the same rates. Similarly, a hotel may offer certain room attributes only on direct channels (more on this in Chapter 16). Part of this rationale is because of the channel cost, effectively setting inventory controls to maximize profitability. But part is also to change customer booking behavior over time. The large chains, and others as well, have put out a few *carrots* to entice direct bookings, such as loyalty points (typically not available for Online Travel Agency (OTA) bookings for example), free Wi-Fi, and member/direct rates. Now add to that list *preferred availability*, which means that a customer may at times finds availability on a direct channel that they do not find on a third-party channel. As with pricing, this inventory approach may not make tactical sense, at least in the short term, but I believe it is a wise move strategically. It can be thought of as an investment in customer engagement; such an investment has a cost, perhaps reduced short-term revenue, but also has a potentially significant upside over time.

These decisions must of course be driven by analytics. The decisions we make and the actions we take need to be aligned with our stated goals, and measured accordingly. Driving bookings to our direct channels is a worthwhile goal, but so is using third-party channels for customer acquisition. If our metrics don't make that distinction (e.g., if we are looking merely at channel mix), we have already failed. In Chapter 14, I'll introduce the *happy/sad litmus test* related to analytics. To oversimplify a bit here, when I see a third-party booking, I'm happy if it is an acquisition, but I may be sad if it is a repeat customer that didn't book direct. Pavan

Kapur, Chief Commercial Officer of Caesars Entertainment, puts it more bluntly, "if a customer books repeatedly on an OTA, you're not doing your job."

Another key aspect of distribution strategy is *onward distribution*. This is not a revenue management function per se, but it is certainly a revenue strategy function. Onward distribution refers to third parties extending rates to customers beyond the intended audience. Perhaps the most extreme example of this is discounted rates that are offered to wholesalers as part of an overall travel package. These discounted rates are bundled with other travel components, such as flights or car rentals, to create a package that the wholesaler sells to the end customer. *But* ... sometimes these discounted rates are offered, either by the selected wholesaler or a partner, as *room-only rates* and not as part of a package; these rates often significantly undercut direct channels, which is clearly not the intended purpose. Matt Busch, Senior Vice President, Equifax, notes that this dynamic also erodes a hotel's returns on paid media, by allowing these lower rates to appear on meta-search next to the hotel's published retail rates. This is a problem facing the hotel industry, particularly smaller chains and independent hotels. Sloan Dean, CEO of Remington Hotels emphasizes that "if you don't get onward distribution right, you don't get revenue management right."

Sloan also makes a larger point that, especially for independent hotels, "distribution strategy and revenue management strategy are one and the same." And Trevor Stuart-Hill, President of Revenue Matters, adds that "for independent hotels, distribution strategy is still the Wild West." The evolution to revenue strategy, which is the focus of this book, necessitates a more holistic view of revenue generation, one that goes well beyond pricing and inventory management. A revenue strategy perspective, which could also be called a commercial strategy perspective, must consider all commercial objectives. Two of these objectives are noted in the preceding paragraphs: loyalty and distribution. Other commercial objectives can include customer acquisition and customer retention. A revenue strategy perspective would mean making pricing and inventory decisions with these objectives in mind as well. For example, such a perspective could call for targeted discounted rates for the purposes of new customer acquisition, as referenced in Chapter 1. These rates must be balanced with other approaches to acquisition of course. Chris Anderson, Professor, Cornell University, emphasized that, with a revenue strategy lens, a focus on distribution (and he includes aspects of digital marketing) may have a meaningfully larger impact on a hotel than a focus on revenue management, and that this is particularly true for independent hotels. Revenue strategy must balance impacts of pricing and inventory with the impacts of digital marketing and paid placement. Chris refers to the latter as the "amazonization of retail, where positioning is critical."

One final point on distribution to close this chapter: as hoteliers, we spend money on *search* to drive direct bookings, but this too requires a revenue strategy lens. We may pay a search engine to drive customers to our direct channels, and in doing so, we can reduce our commission expense, including markup expense. But as we do more of this, and competition drives the price of this search up, we can end up in a place where we pay an amount for search that is similar to what we would have paid in commissions ... so what have we accomplished? Though the immediate value of these two bookings, one via paid search to our own channel and one via an OTA, may be identical, a revenue strategy lens would entail looking beyond the *booking value* to the *acquisition value* of the customer, which is a very different metric and may call for very different decisions.

CHAPTER 9

Merchandising

Rate and Product Presentation

In this chapter, I'll cover two key concepts in merchandising, decoy pricing and choice deferral. These are related to the discipline of revenue management and critical to a more holistic revenue strategy. Merchandising decisions should be led by expert marketers; perhaps, depending on the specific organization, these sit in a discipline other than marketing, such as ecommerce/digital. However, revenue management must be integrally involved. Merchandising is a complex and evolving field (similar to revenue management in that way), and a holistic discussion is beyond the scope of this book, but these two topics in particular, decoy pricing and choice deferral, are inherently linked to revenue management.

Decoy Pricing

There are a few other names for *decoy pricing*, including an academic-sounding *asymmetric dominance*, but I'll stick with decoy pricing. The idea is a simple one: I can present the customer with some options and let them choose what is best for them ... but how could I *influence* that decision with merchandising? Can I steer them toward the option that is best for me (the hotel)? The answer, based on plenty of research, is yes. Let's consider an example: I am selling a standard room for $250 and a suite with breakfast for two for $350. If I wanted to steer the customer toward the suite with breakfast, how could I do that without altering the pricing or features? Easy, I introduce a third option! For example, I could offer the suite without breakfast for $345. Now the suite with breakfast looks like quite a deal. There are several ways to accomplish the same effect; for example, I could offer the suite plus parking for $400. The goal is to make the preferred option, meaning the option that I want the buyer to prefer, look good by comparison, even if the comparison point is one that I don't actually expect to sell.

For reference, there is a fairly well-known example of this from the *Economist* magazine. The magazine was offering an online subscription for $59 and a print and online subscription for $125. They wanted to steer customers to the $125 option. So, they offered a third option: the print subscription for $125. Yes, this really happened, and it worked, and has been well documented by independent sources; a Google search on *Economist decoy pricing* will yield almost 200K results. Customers saw the combination print and online subscription as a *relative* steal and purchased it. Subsequent testing has supported this decision; it turns out that offering an option that no one would buy actually increased revenue! Wow. I believe that there is a great deal of opportunity to apply decoy pricing in the hospitality business, especially for, but certainly not limited to, resort and luxury hotels with a multitude of room types and offerings. The suite with breakfast offer mentioned previously is just one example. In my discussions with Dax Cross, CEO of Revenue Analytics, he suggested that readers of this book should also take a look at the book *Freakonomics* for more insights into consumer psychology. Jason Bryant, Cofounder and CEO, Nor1, emphasizes that decoy pricing, along with approaches like strikethrough pricing, are intended to influence consumer behavior, but they are also intended to ensure that the consumer can easily see the value proposition in the proper context.

Juan Nicolau, Professor of Revenue Management at Virginia Tech, describes the use of attributes to influence consumer behavior well beyond the effect of decoy pricing at a *given* hotel. He emphasized that promotional efforts for certain attributes can influence a consumer's *choice* of hotel. Juan gave an example of a hotel offering a package that included parking, Wi-Fi, and breakfast. Instead of, for example, giving a package pricing discount of $30 (such as $10 off each of these components), the hotel could offer free breakfast. Juan explains that consumers tend to be more attracted to a discount applied to a single attribute (e.g., offering a $30 breakfast for free) than to that same discount applied to a package overall—a clear example of merchandising at work!

Choice Deferral

Another key aspect of merchandising is choice deferral, driven by what economists refer to as *choice overload*, or simply *overchoice*. As hotels offer more and more options to consumers, and seek to provide greater flexibility, this concept will become much more important than it is today. It is too easy to fall into the trap of "providing more choices for the consumer is always good." In his book, *The Paradox of Choice*, psychologist Barry Schwartz explains precisely this. For example, a hotel may offer a standard room, a corner king, and a suite. They may offer each with an advance-purchase rate and a fully refundable retail rate. They may offer a loyalty rate, a breakfast rate, and more. The number of combinations grows exponentially. This is where choice deferral becomes important. To oversimplify: given x number of options (typically 3 or 4), a consumer will select the one that best meets their needs; given x+1 options, the consumer will defer a buying decision. One explanation for this effect is that choice deferral is driven by what economists call *regret anticipation*, meaning the fear of making the wrong choice. More options can actually mean less buying, and there is plenty of research that says so; a Google search on "choice deferral" will yield 4M results. Given the push in hospitality (and many other industries) for flexibility and tailored offerings, this is a real concern. In matters of analytics related to merchandising, I highly recommend testing specifically for this. And if your x becomes too large, you'll need to address this by reducing it through simplified options (in the preceding example, perhaps don't offer the advance-purchase rates on all room types), or by saving and using a consumer's profile/preferences. For example, Jane never eats breakfast at the hotel, so I won't show Jane those rates in the default display.

When Decoy Pricing and Choice Deferral Are at Odds

At this point, astute readers will notice that these two merchandising themes, decoy pricing and choice deferral, *may* be at odds. Specifically, decoy pricing suggests adding more rates for sale, while choice deferral warns against having too many. It is difficult to make a generalization on this point, but I'm going to anyway. Which of these effects matters more? It depends on the nature of the booking and how much time a consumer will devote to the decision. Decoy pricing may have more upside at resort or luxury hotels, as noted earlier, especially for longer lengths of stay and for leisure bookings, where the consumer will devote more time to the booking decision. But for less complex hotels, and especially for business travel, I recommend paying more attention to choice deferral. The opportunity to use a decoy price should of course be considered, but any customer confusion could more than offset any benefit. The risk of choice deferral is real and growing. As the industry gets more comfortable with customer data, and the research on varying consumer preferences grows, we will have the desire to offer more choices, and the technology to enable that. In doing so, we risk making those customer choices more difficult, and some of those choices will likely be deferred. I recommend a robust tracking of bookings (or some proxy such as conversion) as a function of number, and type, of options presented.

The topic of merchandising struck a chord with many of the industry leaders I interviewed for this book. Dax Cross, CEO of Revenue Analytics, suggests that a revenue strategy approach for hotels would entail the development of a recommendation engine that presents something like "top x choices for you," where the x and the choices themselves are personalized. He notes that the auto industry tends to offer many options on new vehicles, but for the number of packages to choose from they typically use $x = 3$, specifically to reduce choice deferral. Craig Eister, former IHG executive, emphasized that the risk of "too many choices" is very real, and that hoteliers need to aggressively reduce choices and tailor those to specific customers or segments of customers. Craig notes that "having too many choices is confusing for the customer AND becomes very difficult to manage as well." Brian Berry, EVP at Pyramid Hotel Group, believes that there is significant untapped upside to hotel companies that can "reduce the chaos" in terms of merchandising. Chris Anderson, Professor at Cornell University notes that the term merchandizing, from a revenue strategy lens, is really behavioral pricing. He also emphasized the need to present "only a very small choice set" to the customer, which becomes even more important, to both customers and hotels, with shrinking booking windows and more mobile bookings.

CHAPTER 10

Total Hotel Revenue Management

Transient, Group, Local Catering, . . . Why Aren't We Better at This?

As noted in Chapter 1, THRM refers to managing demand across multiple revenue streams. In its simplest form, it means managing transient, group, and local catering demand for both sleeping rooms and function space. More advanced THRM involves more revenue streams such as restaurants, outlets, and spas. The nature of THRM, with a more holistic look at hotel revenues and profits, seems to be a logical part of the evolution to revenue strategy. As noted in the introduction to this book, THRM has been on our radar for a *long* time, is seen by many in the discipline as an important opportunity, and has had some significant investments over the years. And yet. . . as an industry, we are not very good at this; several of the industry experts I interviewed echoed this same assessment. In this chapter, I'll briefly cover some key concepts of THRM and point the reader to a white paper that delves into more depth on this topic. Note that, in industry literature, THRM is sometimes referred to as total hotel revenue optimization (THRO).

Why aren't we better at this? Why have we made surprisingly little progress? Two impediments to progress are mentioned in the introduction: differing objectives and lack of quality data. Both are real impediments, but there are others too. I had the privilege of publishing a paper (October 2019) on this very topic with Sherri Kimes, Professor at the National University of Singapore (and formerly Cornell). I refer the reader to that paper: www.hospitalitynet.org, and search on *Kimes Roberts*.

In addition to the impediments of objectives and data noted above, another reason we, as an industry, have not made more progress in

THRM is a practical one: competing priorities. The disciplines that need to be involved, and heavily invested, are revenue management, operations, finance, and information technology (IT). Depending on a company's organizational structure, several other disciplines, such as sales, marketing, and event management, will also need to be involved. At the risk of stating the obvious, each of these disciplines has other important priorities to accomplish; several of the revenue management ones are spelled out in this book. Given the level of complexity in THRM, and the long timelines involved, pushing for and leading such an effort may be a risky career move. I'm reminded of the saying "success has many parents, but failure is an orphan." It would not be unexpected to take on a leadership role in THRM, encounter any number of obstacles, foreseen and not, manage through shifting organizational priorities, lose some executive sponsorship based on the long timeframes involved, and get a blemish (or worse) on your record—a risky proposition indeed.

The topic of THRM certainly struck a chord with many of the experts I interviewed. Andrew Rubinacci, EVP of Revenue Strategy at Aimbridge Hospitality, points out that many large hospitality brand companies are increasingly focused on select service hotels because of their more favorable owner economics, and lower capital investment, especially in a downturn. In addition to having less upside (relative to full-service hotels) in non-room revenue, select service hotels are much more likely to be franchised, and therefore, the brand fees are based primarily on gross room revenue only; this makes the business case for THRM investment a bit tougher. Andrew puts a fine point on this for the large brand companies: development tends to be small and franchised, and brand companies want more flags, so investments in loyalty, for example, may be more appealing.

Kelly McGuire, Managing Principal of Hospitality at ZS Associates, explains why we aren't better at this: "we've made the problem too hard." She continued, "We're trying to optimize across all demand streams when we can't even get decent data from many of them." Instead of framing up a massive optimization problem, Kelly suggests starting much smaller. "Get an analytics culture in the organization, and look for incremental improvements." This requires a commonly understood set of metrics that are tracked, and interpreted regularly, as well as clear communication of performance drivers. Advice from Sherri Kimes, Professor at National

University of Singapore, on how to make progress in THRM was similar, "just start, and start basic." Brian Berry, Executive VP of Commercial Strategy at Pyramid Hotel Group, suggested that the way to approach THRM is to "take a big problem and make it a set of small problems." Sloan Dean, CEO of Remington Hotels, made the analogy to the movie *The Martian*, where Matt Damon's character explains "You solve one problem, and you solve the next one, and then the next. And if you solve enough problems, you get to come home." So, what does this look like? These *small* problems could be: function space management, meeting room assignments, group forecasting, menu engineering, event turn times, and much more. Addressing each of these problems alone can generate meaningful value with a relatively compressed timeline, while addressing many of them together can mean an extremely long payback period for investments. Matt Busch, Senior Vice President, Equifax, notes that "lack of robust data has led to inaction. Revenue strategists of the future will need to be more practical than that." He suggests decomposing the problem "not just by revenue stream but also by capability"; Matt made the analogy to theme parks' simplified pricing and product structure with fast lane/passes—these addressed only a small part of their larger problem, but did so fairly quickly with excellent results.

Despite the challenges and impediments, which are significant, there is a *lot* of money at stake here, and software vendors and intermediaries have sure realized that. Someone will win, and likely win big, in this space. Someone will figure out how to build a base of analytics, probably beginning with simple benchmarking, building to some controlled experiments, and expanding on that in small steps until the much larger THRM problem seems addressable. That *someone* will need a sizable and long-term commitment to fully make THRM a reality, but I'm convinced that the payoff will justify such a commitment. In fact, the continued evolution to revenue strategy requires it.

CHAPTER 11

Revenue Management in a Downturn

Considerations and Specific Actions— Learn From Experience

In this chapter, I'll cover some insights and wisdom I've picked up from the last three downturns, including the pandemic-driven one, as well as some specific steps to take from a revenue strategy perspective. I'll discuss *price wars*, *discount wars*, *grouping up*, and the relative importance of revenue management in a downturn.

Back in 2019, we were in Year 11 of a (mostly) global economic expansion. Then, in early 2020, demand fell off to an extent no one could have imagined. The COVID-19 pandemic had such a devastating impact on travel demand. This impact has been described as greater than the impact of 9/11 and the Global Financial Crisis combined. We may not regain our RevPAR losses, in nominal terms, until perhaps 2024. Though the impacts were not at all equally distributed (e.g., luxury hotels were hit harder, China has recovered faster, nonurban locations fared better, business dropped much more than leisure), these impacts were certainly global. As I write this, vaccine distribution is well underway, though far from uniform, and there is certainly cause for optimism, new variants notwithstanding. Once the virus is contained, or relatively under control, we will be left to dig out of a deep economic recession. Hotels will need to be, and some are, creative in repositioning themselves to go after segments of business that are recovering more rapidly. As an example, hotels that historically have a significant mix of group business will need to become appealing to the transient leisure customer, the latter segment being much more robust in the near term.

We humans have figured out a lot of things, but we have not yet figured out how to defeat the business cycle. After what I hope will be a long and prosperous recovery period, we will have another recession, if history is any guide, the cause and timing of which are of course unknown. I'm reminded of the quote "history doesn't repeat itself, but it rhymes," which is generally attributed to Mark Twain (though there is no written evidence that he actually said this). In any case, history does, and will, *rhyme*; we will have another industry downturn, and in that downturn, reasonable people will do unreasonable things. Humans are emotional creatures. We like to think of ourselves as rational, but we aren't really wired that way. There is an abundance of psychological research, some of it dating back to the 1970s, that says precisely this. We often make choices that defy logic. The reason I mention this here is that we need to be aware of our biases and consciously bring logic to the forefront, as it certainly doesn't always happen by default. Bob Cross, Chairman of Revenue Analytics, explained his version of a common refrain; he emphasized that "desperate times DO NOT call for desperate measures!" He highlighted the need to "bring logic forward."

Numerous studies have shown that demand for an industry can be price inelastic (yes, even in a downturn), while demand for an individual competitor can be price elastic; this is certainly true for the hospitality industry. These two simple facts lead to some predictable outcomes: a) triggering a price war is very short sighted but it will happen and b) price collusion is illegal in many parts of the world ☺.

So, how do we avoid a price war in the next downturn, or even as we climb out of one? Realistically, we don't. Based on a global survey of revenue managers, conducted by Sherri Kimes, Professor at National University of Singapore, and me in May of 2021, 65 percent of respondents indicated that their hotel was a participant in a price war! Ouch. The most common *trigger* for these price wars was generalized panic, though in roughly 30 percent of cases, the price war was triggered by a single rogue hotel. A very common stated reason for dropping prices significantly was to generate cash and be able to pay the bills, especially employee wages. In such cases, short-term survival supersedes longer-term strategy. An important caveat is called for here: if dropping prices actually increases revenue in the short term, then there is a tradeoff between short- and long-term revenue; but dropping prices may or may not lead to increased short-term revenue (this is very case-specific, and warrants evaluation).

Given these results, I don't foresee the industry avoiding a price war in the future. But can we mitigate it somehow? I see two answers to that: a) education and b) game theory. We need more compelling educational materials, perhaps from a leading industry organization, such as HSMAI, that explain exactly what happens in a price war. The downsides are significant and lasting. A steep falloff in rates in a given year can take many years to recover. Furthermore, deep reductions in any given year result in a problem of *reference pricing*. Per Business Dictionary, a reference price is the price that customers "anticipate paying or consider reasonable to pay." If a full-service hotel that typically charges $299/night over the past few years suddenly charges $149/night during a recession, or any low-demand period for that hotel, then this hotel is *worth* $149 in the mind of every customer who paid that amount, and perhaps anyone else who heard about it. Once a downturn ends and recovery begins, it is then difficult to convince that customer that the hotel is worth $299 again. All of this, and much more, should be part of a focused education effort for the industry.

In addition to education, a game theory approach is called for. For those readers unfamiliar with the field of game theory, I recommend reading up on what is perhaps the most famous game theory problem of all: the so-called *prisoner's dilemma*. To simplify a bit, how do you discourage a competitor from significantly dropping rates? You let it be known (through your actions and general public statements; I'm *not* recommending collusion here) that you will follow them down out of necessity. And then you'll need to be ready to back that up. In practice, this is a repeated game of the *prisoner's dilemma*; while the different players cannot coordinate any moves, they certainly can track all past moves, as well as reactions to those moves. I highly recommend a regular audit of price changes for your hotel and each competitor hotel. This is public information, for most retail rates. Larger companies, certainly the large chains, but also large ownership groups or operators, can also push such an audit. A sound general approach in terms of retail pricing in a downturn is "follow down when you need to, perhaps with a lag time, but don't ever lead the way down"; a detailed pricing audit can tell you whether your hotels are actually doing this. To the extent that your hotel has private rates, meaning negotiated, personalized, or otherwise nonpublic, it may be wise to discount those *before* discounting any retail rates.

One important note regarding price wars: the previous downturn (2009) was so long ago that most hotels did not have automated price response models; this time around, many hotels have this in place. What this means is that if each model is using other hotels' retail rates as an input, which they certainly are, we run the risk of a price spiral driven by these very models. Some systems have some safeguards in place, but as an industry, automated price response modeling has never been tested in a downturn until now! Yikes. We need to keep on top of this as an industry. This of course applies to the downturn from the COVID-19 pandemic, and the recovery, but more broadly, it applies to any timeframe in which any market is experiencing weak demand. This makes the audits, mentioned earlier, critically important. One word of caution in terms of following down in rate; while it is important to demonstrate a clear strategy of following down, to reduce the incentive for a competitor to lead the way down, some leeway is called for in terms of interpreting information (in this case, price shopping data). It is too easy to say some version of "you're only as smart as your dumbest competitor." While there is some truth to this, it often misses some context. Sometimes, hotels lower retail rates because of something specific to that hotel, for example, a large cancelation, or even because of a mistake. These should not immediately be considered the first strikes in a price war. For this reason, I think a reasonable approach is to follow down but with a lag time of perhaps a few days. In this context, price changes are less likely to be *overinterpreted* as salvos in a price war. To state the (perhaps) obvious, this dynamic does not go away when demand begins to recover. Globally, we will be in a soft demand environment for a few years, and locally, this of course happens all the time. Cindy Estis Green, CEO and Cofounder of Kalibri Labs, has done some interesting research showing that recovery timeframes, in terms of RevPAR recovery, are shorter for hotels that resist a deep discounting approach. Specifically, holding rate relative to your competitors in soft demand times can result in reduced occupancy and reduced RevPAR, but the recovery for these hotels is much more robust than for those that chose a deep discounting approach. This is a clear example of a strategic approach to revenue management!

In addition to avoiding a price war, we need to avoid a *discount war* (that's a term that I made up as I wrote this book). To oversimplify a bit, here's what happens in a downturn in the hospitality industry: people panic, and in a panic, people do illogical things. If panic leads to poor decision making, then extreme panic can lead to extremely poor decision making. Sherri Kimes, Professor at National University of Singapore, notes that Rule #1 in a downturn is "don't panic." To that, I'll add my snarky caveat and say: panic all you want, just don't act on that ☺. I'll rephrase here the caveat from earlier in the chapter: it is possible, but not at all a given, that aggressive discounting could increase short-term revenue. If that is the case in a specific situation, then you'll need to balance short-term goals with longer-term goals. When I refer to acting on panic, I mean letting emotion take over and doing something that is impulsive and can lead to reduced short-term revenue.

In the coming months and years, there will be plenty of meetings about demand generation, and in those meetings, lots of ideas will be put forth. Some of these ideas will be good, some will be mediocre, and some will be dreadful. It is critical that all such ideas are vetted. In a downturn, it is pretty difficult to generate overall demand, and most ideas tend to be geared toward stealing share. The problem with that category of ideas is that they are often very easily matched. To the extent that these share-stealing ideas involve discounted rates, we will have just triggered a discount war. Offering new or deeper advance-purchase rates, deeper discounts on loyalty rates, more or deeper account rates, or any number of similar ideas is likely to trigger a competitive response, resulting in a net revenue loss. In addition, as a reminder, any discounted rates should meet the two criteria described in Chapter 6, with special emphasis on Condition #2 (a price-sensitive audience). One more word of caution on this topic: Beware a false sense of activity! Regardless of your position or discipline, there will be enormous pressure to show that you are *doing something*! As an aside, this is true anytime demand is lower than a given stakeholder thinks it ought to be, but especially so in a broad downturn. I encourage you to resist the urge to add an item to your list just because your "what we are doing" list looks too short. If demand is down significantly, there is no mitigation plan that will fully offset that, even if the next downturn is mild. Here too, an audit is called for. Relative to the 2009 downturn, we as an industry have made remarkable progress in our ability to benchmark against our competition. There are now data providers that can help a hotel or set of hotels understand their performance by channel and segment relative to their competition, and this information can be used to conduct audits on discounting. This is a new capability for the industry—*new* meaning not available in the previous downturns/recoveries. For example, is my competition opening up new discount segments and selling significant volume? If so, I may need to follow in the same way I would if the competition was lowering their retail rates. This is analogous to the pricing strategy for retail rates; with regard to discount rates, I should not lead the way down, but I should be prepared to follow quickly.

What about *grouping up* (mostly for full-service hotels)? The term *grouping up* refers to hotels' efforts to book many more group RN than they typically would, often from customer segments that are more price-sensitive than those the hotel typically targets. This is admittedly an odd topic to bring up right now, given that the nature of the pandemic-induced downturn (health concerns with large gatherings) means that the group segment may be slow to recover. However, I'm very optimistic about the recovery of the group segment. I was a guest on Klaus Kohlmayr's IDeaS podcast *Unconstrained Conversations* where I explained the reasoning for my optimism, and I mention it here because the topic presents a good example of the evolution from revenue management to revenue strategy. For many hotels, grouping up is a common response to a threat of softening transient demand, and it makes sense, though admittedly less so at the time this book is going to print. The problem is that *group up* is somewhat of a platitude. Hotels should always group up if doing so drives performance, regardless of our position in any demand cycle. For a group up strategy, I believe the first step is to revisit a hotel's forecast. By this, I mean not just a transient demand forecast, which by nature is relatively short term. Hotels that have any meaningful amount of group business have some sort of system or process or heuristic that drives group pricing, all of which are driven in part by a demand projection. As the probability of a soft demand timeframe changes, these projections should be revisited, and perhaps adjusted to reflect realistic risk. For example, if my hotel is projecting an overall demand level in the next 12 months that is similar to current demand levels, and yet market indicators suggest a significant demand recovery in the next 12 months, I should probably adjust my forecast upward. To the extent that I have a process/model/heuristic in place that recommends pricing based in part on such a forecast, my pricing will likely increase because of this forecast adjustment. For large hotel companies, or owners and operators of multiple hotels, such a validation could be accomplished, relatively easily, with a centralized audit. And now, thanks to data/analytics providers such as Kalibri Labs, TravelClick, and STR, such information is readily available, even for individual hotels. A risk adjustment to the forecast will result in risk-adjusted pricing for the group segment. The reason this approach is much better, in my view, than a more generic group up strategy, is that softening or strengthening demand is not at all uniform—it will vary by market (some markets are more recession resistant), and it will vary by timeframe (highly seasonal markets may be more recession resistant in peak times, for example). This approach to grouping up aligns with an overall theme of revenue management: get your forecast right, and then apply analytics and/or modeling to pricing and inventory decisions.

Value of RM in a Downturn

If you are a revenue management leader, you may be asked some version of "why do we need revenue management in a downturn? Don't we just open everything up?" I've heard this myself in each of the last two downturns, and am hearing it now of course. In short, I believe that in a downturn, inventory management decisions matter less (but they do matter), while pricing decisions may matter more. Here's why. Inventory management decisions matter the most when forecasted occupancies approach a sellout; the number of sellout nights during a downturn is most certainly not zero, at least not for extended periods. In fact, the percentage of sellout nights in the 2009 downturn was roughly half of the percentage of sellout nights during peak years. That figure was of course much lower for 2020, but will not be as the recovery builds in 2022 and beyond. So, inventory management in a downturn could be considered roughly *half as important* as opposed to unimportant.

Pricing decisions, on the other hand, may matter more in a downturn. The reason for this is that pricing mistakes can be masked by strong demand.

If I overprice or underprice during a portion of the booking window, I can mostly, but not entirely, recover from that in the face of strong demand. If I overprice, and lose some bookings, my forecast will reflect that, and my pricing will be adjusted down a bit for future bookings. Conversely, if I underprice, I'll have a surge in bookings, and my forecast will rise, triggering a price increase. All of this is predicated on a strong demand environment. In a downturn, this mitigating effect is muted. As Brian Berry, Executive VP of Commercial Strategy at Pyramid Hotel Group, describes pricing decisions in a downturn, "your margin of error becomes increasingly thin."

Of course, this effect is highly dependent on some assumptions on price sensitivity, forecast accuracy, and competitive response. But let me describe a series of simulations I ran involving underpricing in two different scenarios, one with excess demand and one with excess capacity. For this exercise, I used a hypothetical 100-room hotel, with a fairly standard *S-shaped* price response function (similar to those introduced in Chapter 5), and assumed one-night stays with a perfect forecast and no changes or cancellations (if only the real world would cooperate ☺). I also assumed perfect adherence to the systems' price recommendations. For the scenario with demand less than capacity, the optimal price, in my particular simulation, was $120, for each day of the booking window. If I underprice for a portion of the window, I see no recovery in rate. In this example, I underpriced for 30 percent of the booking window (meaning a portion when I saw 30 percent of demand), and underpriced by 30 percent (meaning my actual price was 30 percent below what the model recommended). The result, after that period of underpricing, was that my optimal price for the remainder of the booking window was $120 again—exactly what it would have been had I not underpriced earlier. So, this underpricing cost me dearly, and there was no rate recovery. Conversely, in a scenario with demand in excess of capacity, I do see some rate recovery. Using the same assumptions as earlier, I ran this simulation. Because of the high demand, and higher market prices, the optimal rate in my simulation was $145 for each day of the booking window. But now if I underprice, again, by 30 percent for 30 percent of the booking window, I see that the model recognizes this, and accounts for the excess demand by raising the optimal price. In this particular simulation, the optimal price for the remainder of the booking window (the part after the period of underpricing) jumped to $168. The reason it went above the original

$145 is because of the capacity constraint. So, in this case, underpricing still hurt me, but I was able to recoup some of that loss. These particular simulation results are just to make a point. Actual results, or results of your own simulations, will be dependent on the factors mentioned earlier, as well as where in the booking window the mispricing occurs, how fast it is detected and acted upon, how the forecast adjusts, and so on. For those so inclined, I recommend running a few of these simulations yourselves. If you find anything intriguing, I'd love to hear about it. I've run several different scenarios like this, because I think that's what nerdy professors are supposed to do. I'll share one more interesting finding from this simulation exercise: a mistake early in the booking window is less damaging than a mistake later in the booking window, all else being equal. As an aside, this is a lesson that goes well beyond pricing and applies to much of business (and more): if you're going to make a mistake, make it early!

For more context on revenue management in a downturn, the following photo is from a 2009 notebook and shows the type of things that we were thinking about in revenue management, at least the subset that

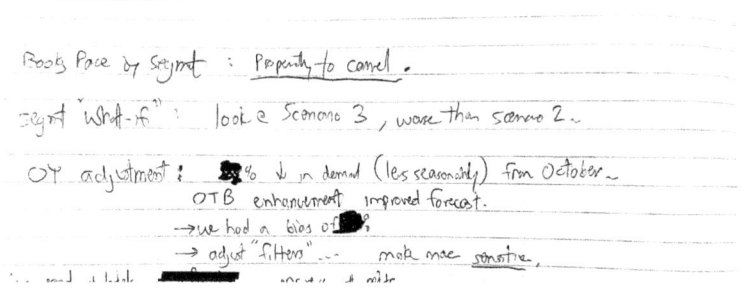

Figure 11.1 Notes from a downturn

appeared on this particular page:

You can see that we were looking at accuracy (technically, predictive power) of our group bookings, in this case, trying to predict our cancelations. Given the severity of the 2009 downturn, it is not surprising that we added an *even worse* scenario, as noted. We also looked at making adjustments to our demand forecast. The *OY* here stands for one yield, which is Marriott's proprietary RMS. It is powered by a type of forecast called a *time-series forecast*, which is a fancy way of saying that it takes the past and uses it to predict the future, with some adjustments. A time-series forecast will eventually *catch up* to a dramatic change in demand;

the reason for an adjustment is to speed that process up. Much more on forecasting can be found in Chapter 3. In Chapter 3, we discussed the importance of communicating a forecast, and probably a few forecast scenarios, to your key stakeholders. This is more important than ever in a downturn. When stakeholders disagree on plans and actions, it is often because they disagree on the forecast. Also remember that a weak forecast does not automatically mean you should lower prices. This is sometimes called the *Sunday fallacy*, in reference to Sunday nights at most hotels; as noted in Chapter 5, they are often low occupancy, but lowering rate significantly will drive only a small increase in RN.

If there is a single theme to this chapter, *Revenue Management in a Downturn*, it is this: avoid doing things based on emotion. If you are hell-bent on doing that, please wait for the recovery ☺ (see the next chapter).

CHAPTER 12

Revenue Management in a Recovery

A Seldom-Discussed Time in the Business Cycle for Revenue Management

As this book goes to print, we are likely to be in the relatively early stages of a fairly lengthy recovery. In this chapter, I'll share some learnings from the past two recoveries, discuss how to gradually undo the damage of a price war or a discount war, and when it is appropriate to take pricing risks or inventory risks to drive rate and revenue in a recovery.

As noted in the previous chapter, history tends to *rhyme*. If it continues to do so, and I suspect it will, then we will be in a recovery period postpandemic. This holds for the economy overall as well as for the travel industry. As the economy recovers, and lodging demand recovers correspondingly, hotel RevPARs will recover as well. But are there things we can do to hasten that recovery? That is a rhetorical question—if not, I would have excluded this chapter from the book ☺. There are two themes from the previous chapter that I'd like to revisit here: price (and discount) wars and mistakes.

Price (and discount) *wars*: The italics is because what we're really talking about here is the opposite of a war, but the same principles apply. The value of pricing audits, as described in Chapter 11, for your own hotel as well as your competitors' hotels, is significant here too. Recall a pricing strategy theme from Chapter 11: don't lead the way down, but follow when you need to, which is almost always. In a recovery, the inverse is true: lead the way up, and follow, rapidly, when you can—this means always, with the rarest of exceptions. And a detailed pricing audit will help you understand if your hotels are actually doing this. For example, are there hotels, dates, or timeframes, perhaps in certain portions of a booking window, where I see I am not leading up and not following up, at least not rapidly enough? This can all be done using existing retail price shopping data. Similarly, a *discount audit*, as described earlier, will help you understand if your hotels are closing out discounted rates at least as aggressively as the competition. As a reminder, this is a new capability relative to the previous economic cycle. This part will take a bit more work than the retail pricing audit. A data/solution provider could help lead the way here, including helping with the assessment of the impact of such segment yielding approaches. The overall theme here is to lead up and follow up, both in pricing and in inventory controls, and to put some tracking/audits in place to ensure that we are actually doing that at the hotel level.

Mistakes: This is also in italic, because I'm not advocating making mistakes. But I *am* suggesting taking risks, and this will certainly lead to some mistakes (or else they wouldn't be called risks). By *risks*, in this context, I'm referring to pricing and inventory risks. For example, if my retail price recommendation engine says $199 for a given future date (and it is set up properly and I trust it completely), but I want to lead up, I may want to try $229. This should, at least initially, be done on lower risk timeframes such as over portions of the booking window when you don't put a lot of bookings at risk, but your pricing direction is of course clear and public. Or if you have a particularly strong base of business, perhaps group, contract, negotiated transient, or even promotional bookings, then you could take some retail *rate risk* without taking on undue revenue risk. I recommend taking these rate risks early in the booking window; as noted in the previous chapter, mistakes made early are more easily mitigated.

Taking inventory risks can be thought of in a somewhat similar way. The expression *taking inventory risks* means yielding discount segments more aggressively than your current segment-level forecast would suggest. There is one crucial difference between rate risks and inventory risks. Unlike retail price positioning, inventory management decisions are not public, and so there is no signaling advantage, meaning you can't take some action that can then be easily noticed and followed. With inventory risks, we are talking about yielding discount segments more aggressively than a system would recommend; in this case, let's assume that the demand forecast is accurate, and the desired mix of business is a straightforward calculation. Though there is no signaling effect, there are two reasons to take such an inventory risk: forecast optimism, and segment shift. In a recovery scenario, demand will at times come in stronger than a system forecast suggests. Recall that these systems use a time-series forecast, projecting the past into the future with some adjustments, details of which are in Chapter 3. A recovery implies some inflection point(s) where demand will take an unexpected upturn. Taking inventory risk, then, in effect means making inventory management decisions based on an upward revision of the current forecast, or at least the potential upward revision. If these risks are taken early in the booking window, any resulting mistake can be somewhat mitigated. The second reason to take some inventory risk has to do with segment shift. As noted in Chapter 6, bookings for every discount segment can be represented by a pie chart, where one section is *incremental*, and the other section is *tradedown*. Taking inventory risk can reflect some optimism for potential segment shift. As discussed in Chapter 6, when a discount rate is closed, those customers who would have booked it can either book a higher rate at the same hotel, or they can go elsewhere (or not go). If a discount segment is highly incremental, those customers are unlikely to book a higher rate at the same hotel (by definition). On the other hand, if some significant portion of those customers are trading down from retail rate, then closing the discount would result in many of those customers booking the retail rate. And if you have reason to believe that your competition is reducing availability of similar discount rates, the likelihood of these customers *trading up* to retail increases. As noted before, any mistakes made early are more easily mitigated. To connect a couple of themes here, specifically, this chapter to Chapter 8, another way to increase the likelihood of your customers trading up to retail at your hotel is to provide them with a compelling loyalty program, and therefore a strong incentive to do so.

One theme for this chapter, and the preceding one, is that a strategic approach to revenue management is especially beneficial in times of inflection. These inflection points are certainly driven by economic cycles, and of course by disruption events that trigger them. But more broadly, inflection points are quite common in any given market, and these same principles apply. As the discipline continues to evolve to revenue strategy, and technology plays an increasingly significant role in tactical decisions, it is precisely at such inflection points where human intervention matters most.

CHAPTER 13

Machine Learning in Revenue Management

What It Is and How It Will Shape the Discipline; It's Not (Just) About the Math

The impact of *machine learning* on revenue management will explode in the coming years, and I can't imagine writing a book on revenue management without addressing it. In this chapter, I'll give a brief overview of machine learning, and how it applies to various aspects of revenue management, and more broadly to the industry, as well as a look to the future.

Regardless of your role, discipline, or level, you will likely be asked something like "how can we use machine learning to get better at___?" My suggested answer is something like "we can use machine learning to make this discipline (or department, division, . . .) better, and derive more value; the key is to find specific problems that lend themselves to a machine learning approach." At the risk of another platitude, machine learning will transform most functions of most industries; in several industries, it already has. If your job has not been specifically impacted by machine learning, it likely will be.

I had a consultant (company name withheld) in my office who said "I want to talk about how we can get machine learning into Marriott revenue management." My reply caught him off guard. "What type of machine learning, and what aspects of revenue management do you have in mind?" Uhhh. . . Without a thoughtful response, I politely sent him on his way. My point in telling this story is as a warning: there are a lot of "experts" out there selling machine learning approaches for all sorts of business applications, a point echoed by most people I interviewed for this book. As an aside, a friendly note to vendors: please do your homework; when I met with this gentleman, Marriott had already been using machine learning in our RMS for almost a year ☺. I didn't expect him to know that, but I also didn't expect him to assume otherwise.

Some context is warranted: what are we talking about? What is machine learning? Machine learning is a subset of Artificial Intelligence (AI). Broadly speaking, AI is any application of a machine imitating a human, from a kiosk at McDonalds to a sophisticated recommendation engine on Amazon. Machine learning is a set of techniques that allow a computer to get better at its task, based on "experience" ("experience" to a machine means data). While machine learning has been around since the 1950s, its recent explosion has been primarily driven by two factors: a) data (availability, and labeling/tagging), and b) computing power. There are three broad categories of machine learning models. One is directly applicable to revenue management: so called *supervised models*. Just for fun, the other two categories are called *unsupervised models* (often used for clustering and segmentation), and *reinforcement models* (often used for targeting and recommendation engines). As an aside, some specialists add a fourth category, called *semi-supervised models*. I should note here that any of these categories can be useful to revenue management, though "supervised" models are likely more immediately applicable. The term "supervised" refers to the fact that these models have targets and they have answers; the goal of these models is to predict things, and then learn from any prediction errors.

At this point in the chapter, I hope the first revenue management application has become obvious: demand forecasting. Forecasting is perfectly suited to a machine learning approach, specifically a supervised model approach. With demand forecasting, the goal is quite clear, the data is readily available, and the quality of each forecast is objectively apparent. These characteristics are what make forecasting a great fit for machine learning. The same holds true for cancellation forecasting, and more broadly, a great deal of predictive analytics.

While forecasting clearly lends itself to a machine learning approach, the same cannot (yet) be said for inventory management. Sloan Dean, CEO of Remington Hotels, points to machine learning as a way to "make *some* portions of revenue management better." Inventory management is a math problem, one that can be solved explicitly with techniques from the field of Operations Research. Note that I'm referring to the modeling part here; there is quite a lot of complexity to inventory management on property, from inventory balancing to same day selling, to changes in departure dates, and much more. The role of an inventory manager is as complicated as it is critical. It is not immediately obvious how machine learning could help with inventory management (caveat: if the industry ever gets to full customer-centric inventory management, I'll retract this statement ☺).

What about machine learning for pricing? I'll answer that with a qualified yes. The answer is certainly yes, meaning that machine learning is of course applicable to (and currently used for) pricing, and there is significant upside opportunity here. Just as forecast models can be evaluated in near-real time, and adjusted accordingly, so too can price response models. The models used to predict a customer's price response lend themselves to a machine learning approach. For example, a customer's response to a given price may be a function of several different factors, in unforeseen combinations. Models that incorporate this can provide more predictive value. As noted in the introduction, we knowingly make pricing and inventory decisions that do not maximize hotel profits, for the sake of loyalty, channel strategy, or some other reason (employee rates or owner rates, for example). Looking ahead, a modeling approach that explicitly accounts for these sometimes-competing interests may be a major step forward for this discipline, and a machine learning algorithm is likely to be at the center of this.

Dax Cross, CEO of Revenue Analytics, notes that machine learning models are already being used to measure price elasticity today, and feels strongly that they can be adapted to be more targeted across various pricing decisions and customer segments. Jason Bryant, Cofounder and CEO, Nor1, connected machine learning to the topic of overrides first discussed in Chapter 1, and in more detail in Chapter 5. Specifically, he notes that the extensive use of overrides can make machine learning less effective; the machine can make recommendations but can only "learn" about how to improve those recommendations if those recommendations are implemented. Even in such cases, machine learning is still valuable—it's just that the learning itself is hampered. Jason also pointed out that "pricing hotel rooms is a whole lot less complex than driving a car, and machines are getting quite good at the latter." Craig Eister, former IHG executive, emphasized that an important role for a revenue manager of the future is to "help the machine learn." Machine learning can also be useful in discounting decisions. In fact, Bain & Company's white paper (Bringing Order to Discounts Gone Haywire, May 2020), referenced in Chapter 6, addresses precisely this topic.

At this point, you may be wondering why I used the word "qualified" when answering yes earlier in the chapter. I certainly believe in the value that machine learning could bring to pricing models. But, based on my numerous interviews for this book, I'm not convinced that a lack of machine learning is the primary constraint in the effectiveness of pricing models (at least not yet in most organizations). I believe that user adoption is the primary constraint; more details of this are in Chapter 5. Of course, different organizations are in different places in terms of system adoption. If your organization is comfortable with the level of adoption, then you should focus your attention on making the models better, and machine learning can play a big role. I should also note the possibility (probability) that using machine learning to improve pricing models may also improve trust and therefore system adoption.

Merchandising is also ripe for machine learning. The display and presentation of rates and offerings, along with the tracking of user interaction (searches, views, and hopefully bookings), lend themselves to a machine learning approach. You can envision a machine determining in real time the combination of rates, inventory, display, and presentation that will maximize conversion, or bookings, or revenue, or any other desired metric. The machine will constantly tweak these variables and learn which combinations are better than others. This is not a futuristic view; in fact, the retail industry has been doing this for many years, and other industries have followed. Despite some notable progress, the hospitality industry tends to lag here, a theme echoed by many of the experts I interviewed for this book. Stated reasons for this lag are many, from a lack of broad understanding of machine learning to limited investment capacity to many competing priorities.

Chris Anderson, Professor, Cornell University, offered an important word of caution about the use of machine learning. He says that machine learning is "very myopic," adding that "machine learning is great for myopic problems with no strategic implications." This includes forecasting and price response, but, at least for now, excludes revenue management implications for distribution, loyalty, and even competitive response. Machines don't (yet) do strategy!

One impediment to translating the potential value of machine learning into actual business value is a lack of broad understanding of the topic. Some people may be intimidated by the topic, perhaps because many explanations get very technical. Others may believe they understand it when they don't. It is human nature to overestimate our understanding of things, and machine learning is no exception. I know this to be true because I'm guilty of it myself. I began studying machine learning around 2017. At the time, I was pretty sure I knew a lot about it. I have a graduate degree in Operations Research, have written plenty of code, and consider myself a nerd. However, I was wrong. I didn't really understand it. Since then, I've taken two online courses in machine learning, read a lot about it, built some models (both supervised and unsupervised), and I'm most certainly at the beginner (perhaps advanced beginner) stage.

There is a fairly common misperception about machine learning: you take an enormous database and plug it into a powerful computer and hit "go," and then the computer tells you what to do. This is, at least for the foreseeable future, firmly in the realm of science fiction. In the real world, a machine still needs instructions. These instructions can include tradeoffs—specifically, how to balance often competing objectives. To use an Operations Research perspective: the human needs to set the objective function and the constraints. And humans will always need to prioritize efforts; we can use machine learning techniques to improve our models, but should we focus our modeling efforts, for example, on paid search effectiveness or on the impact of an expanded cancellation policy? These are not easy questions. Business leaders in all disciplines and at all levels need to educate themselves about machine learning, beyond sound bites and platitudes. Those that do so will be well positioned to lead their organizations, and will be able to capitalize on its enormous potential value.

As noted throughout this book, the evolution to revenue strategy will, among other things, entail technology's increasing role in tactical decisions of revenue management. And these tactical decisions will be increasingly driven by machine learning. A word of advice for anyone in revenue management, and actually anyone in any business function in any industry: study up on machine learning. You do not need to be an expert practitioner, but you will need to understand the basics, and be able to think through how this applies to a wide variety of business problems. Put another way, using the same foreign language analogy we saw in Chapter 9, you don't need to be *fluent* in machine learning, but you will need to be *conversational*.

CHAPTER 14

Topline Analytics

Performance Management, Evaluation, Actionable Insights

In this chapter, I'll cover some key concepts of analytics that apply to revenue generation, from pursuing a goal other than short-term profit maximization to performance analytics and activity assessments to testing and business case reviews. As noted in the introduction to the book, the evolution from revenue management to revenue strategy necessitates involvement in all aspects of revenue generation, guided by analytics. This chapter will delve deeper into that.

The phrase *Topline Analytics* is purposefully quite broad. As noted in Chapter 1, revenue management should be integrally involved in all revenue decisions. This is certainly true for pricing and inventory decisions that directly impact other disciplines, and the larger goals of the organization. Some obvious examples of such goals include customer acquisition and retention, loyalty, and distribution. As noted in Chapter 8, many decisions that are made on behalf of hotels, or sets of hotels, may not be profit maximizing in the short term, and these decisions often involve matters of pricing and inventory management. As referenced in Chapter 2, the goal of revenue management has evolved from revenue maximization to profit maximization to a more nebulous sounding *benefit maximization*, and today's revenue managers must operate with this context at the heart of everything they do. This may necessitate what appears to be sub-optimal pricing in the pursuit of acquiring a customer with a high potential future value. It may also entail *giving* things to guests that could easily warrant a fee, in the pursuit of driving customer engagement and loyalty. Finally, this benefit maximization goal may call for restricting inventory on some channels, even at the cost of bookings, in pursuit of a holistic distribution strategy. My point here is that these pricing and inventory decisions necessarily involve tradeoffs, balancing the sometimes-conflicting interests of acquiring new customers, driving loyalty, supporting a longer-term distribution strategy, and of course generating profitable revenue in the immediate term. Revenue management, as it evolves to revenue strategy, must be at the *center* of these decisions.

Performance Analytics

One critical area where the discipline of revenue management must lead is *performance analytics*. By this, I mean analytics related to performance management, as opposed to analytics in support of targeted marketing, for example. Performance management is at the heart of what revenue management departments at large ownership groups do. Erich Jankowski, VP of Commercial Strategy at Host Hotels, notes that an owner, who is often not the operator, or an asset manager is typically very tuned in to major decisions related to demand generation and demand management. In this sense, I believe they aren't really revenue management departments; they are well on their way to becoming revenue strategy departments.

The discipline of revenue management needs to be the center of topline performance management. It is too easy, and quite common, for analytics functions to produce a great deal of reporting; this is true at all levels of organizations. This reporting is a very tangible output, and some of it is useful. That said, a word of caution here: beware a false sense of reporting! It is enticing, and even addictive, for a revenue manager or analyst to generate and pore over lots of detailed reports, be able to recite various statistics, and generally have a solid command of all significant revenue metrics. However, this is not the same as really understanding performance *drivers* for the hotel, and such reporting may or may not lead to specific decisions. This is a point that is easy to underappreciate. I like to use the *Happy/Sad* litmus test; when I read a report about the performance of a hotel or set of hotels, I want to know if I should be happy or sad. Now that I've phrased it this way, you may be reflecting on all of the reporting you personally receive; do you know from a given report or set of reports if you should be happy or sad? Do you know if you should be doing anything differently? Based on my numerous interviews for this book, the answer is very likely to be *no*. An abundance of reporting can lead to a false sense of security, and more specifically, a false sense of control. This *Happy/Sad* litmus test could be used for *all* exception reporting. For example, you may want to look at any hotel, among the set of hotels for which you have an interest, that has declined more than 10 percent in group RN versus the previous year. On the surface, this seems useful. But that 10 percent threshold may catch a few hotels with low volumes, and therefore high variability in the percent-change figure. That threshold may also catch some hotels where being down more than 10 percent in group RN is a good idea, and conversely, miss hotels that *should* be down in group volume but aren't, for example, if there is much higher-rated transient demand. This example is broadly applicable to other segments of business as well. In fact, other than the retail and premium segments, it is not immediately obvious that an increase or decrease in segment level volume should make one happy or sad. . . Similarly, other than direct channel bookings, it is not immediately obvious that an increase or decrease in channel-level volume should make one happy or sad. . . This is where a talented business analyst is crucial; it is also where an abundance of reporting may be a hindrance.

To give one example of why a talented business analyst is crucial, consider the following scenario: a common mistake in revenue analytics in hospitality (also true for most industries, I presume), usually directed at some measure of weak performance, is this: xx percent of the aggregate performance is driven by only (small number) hotels; fix these hotels and you fix the issue. To make this point clearer, let's consider an example: I'm analyzing an aggregate of 20 hotels, with a combined revenue decline versus last year of 7 percent, or approximately $28M. I need to *tell a story* to my stakeholders. Here goes: "These 20 hotels are down $28M, but that is entirely driven by just two hotels, one of which is down $14.5M, and the other down $13.5M." Details on this example are in Appendix 2, but I'll get to the point now: the statement is factually correct, but *highly* misleading. Hotels #4 and #13 (see Appendix 2) do have a combined revenue loss of $28M. But is that the full story? It turns out that 12 of the 20 hotels have lost revenue versus last year! Furthermore, while the two largest decliners *explain* the entire loss, the same can be said for the next three; those three have a combined loss of $31M. Similarly, the four after that could *explain* the total loss, with their combined loss of $32M. The takeaway here: do *not* use percentages of a total if any of the individual numbers can be negative. This is exceedingly common and quite misleading (full disclosure: I've done it myself in moments of confusion and weakness), and is an example of why a talented and insightful analyst is key.

Assessment of Activities

In addition to performance management analytics, and associated reporting, another area of focus for revenue management is the assessment of the activities of the hotel or organization. Let's say we have spent a lot of time and money executing some demand generation activity (a promotion, for example); should we keep doing that, or should we alter course, or should we abandon it altogether? Recall the discussions of dilution and displacement from Chapter 2; these concepts should be applied, and clearly explained, to *any* assessment of activities, including any testing (more on this in a moment). Assessments grounded in analytics should help a hotel or organization decide which activities to pursue. And yet, I have read far too many articles that give some version of "assess your segments to see which are growing and shrinking, and then plan your sales and marketing activities accordingly." This is an example of the *lazy wording* discussed in Chapter 1.

Andrew Rubinacci, EVP, Revenue Strategy, Aimbridge Hospitality, emphasized the need for alignment on goals and metrics. He says "it comes down to education—it took us 20 years for RPI to be ingrained. Driving RPI is easy. You can buy RevPAR through third-party channels, but it may not be very profitable. Channels have changed, and metrics need to as well." Andrew specifically mentioned *The Kalibri Vision*, meaning that we as an industry need to manage our segments and channels holistically, and that we need to align owners, operators, and brands on this. I love this quote from Andrew: "anyone we pay, we may want to constrain," a not-so-subtle nod toward aggressive channel management.

Testing

In business, we test a lot of things to see if they are working. Testing should be a very prominent part of analytics. *A/B testing* is quite common in many aspects of business, and you may see the results of such testing in your daily routine, from the headlines you read to the design of the websites you visit, and even in your Facebook feed. For a more detailed look at A/B testing, in the context of evaluating discount rates, including its limitations, please refer to Chapter 6.

Another word of caution: beware a *false sense of testing*! Here's how that can play out: you and I are having a debate. I want to implement a specific promotion, believing it will drive more customers to the hotel. You believe that this promotion will actually lose money because the only customers who will act on it are existing customers. We debate back and forth, and neither of us can convince the other to change their mind. So ... "ok, let's test it." Aha, the path of least resistance. I've seen this too many times to count, and the experts I interviewed for this book echo this assessment. But seriously, who can be against testing such things? Actually, *everyone* should be against it, unless and until the test is clearly defined. There is *only one* situation where something should be called a test: if it is actually a test! More specifically, this means that there is something, or a set of things, that: a) we do not know, b) is important to know, and c) the test will let us know. When you read this, it sounds patently obvious. But in practice, this is not straightforward at all. Before conducting any test, I highly recommend aligning on exactly what is being tested, specifically what do we not know that we should know that the test will tell us, as well as what a conclusive test result would look like. Based on numerous conversations I've had across many companies, including beyond the hospitality industry, the approach described is frighteningly uncommon. Ever the optimist, I'll call this upside opportunity.

There is an important psychological aspect to such assessments as well. An analytics team can't really be a good partner to a marketing team, if the analytics team takes the position of "do whatever you want, and then we will analyze it and tell you how well you did." Based on my interviews, this dynamic is fairly common in the industry, especially so for large organizations. It seems pretty obvious that this approach will lead to lack of trust and eventually lack of communication. And of course, this leads to a lack of actual assessment. The people doing the demand generation work and the people doing the analytics of that work need to operate as one (pardon the cliché). This means aligning upfront on what measurements and analysis will take place and under what conditions our actions will be adjusted.

Business Case Reviews

Finally, business case reviews represent an important, and growing, aspect of analytics. Again, I see upside opportunity; translation: we're not as good as we need to be. This opportunity is also a common theme from other industry veterans I've spoken with. Many hospitality companies, from brand companies to owners to operators to vendors, have made some significant technology investments recently, including websites, apps, data platforms, personalization engines, analytics tools, and much more. These were all (presumably) predicated on a business case. But assumptions in a business case often don't hold up over time, especially if the time horizon involved spans more than a year or so. Some of these investments have paid off handsomely, others, not so much. My point here is that the evaluation of many of these business cases, from the upfront alignment on success metrics to the assessment of the steady-state impact, should be led by a revenue strategy function. Based on my interviews for this book, this evaluation is lacking, especially on the back end, meaning *postmortems*. There are some valid reasons for this, particularly prioritization. Rationalizations can sound like this: "the new system is in place and working; why would I spend my limited time and resources fine-tuning the business case? I should be focused on the future." On the surface, this rationalization seems sound. However, it misses a critical point: business case reviews after a project is completed present a unique and powerful learning opportunity. If a project didn't achieve the stated goals, why not? Were the assumptions flawed, and if so, how did that happen? Was there another dynamic involved that impacted the results but that was not considered in the original business case, and if so, how did we miss that? And on and on. They key is to *learn* from the evaluation. If original assumptions didn't hold up, is it possible that there was some *unconscious bias* involved? Note that the term unconscious bias certainly applies to social and demographic matters; however, it also applies to business strategy and decision making, which is a point I emphasized in the Business Strategy course I taught at Virginia Tech. If a certain dynamic impacted results, but was not part of the upfront case, perhaps it should have been, and understanding why is a tremendous learning opportunity. Many *surprises* should not be surprises, especially true for competitive reactions. OK, I'm off my soapbox on business case reviews.

As we evolve toward revenue strategy, we will be making critical decisions on metrics, goal-setting, and resource allocation. These decisions must be guided largely, though not exclusively, by analytics, and those analytics will certainly encompass performance management, testing, and activity assessments. All of this will need to be clearly communicated (no *lazy wording* allowed) and updated as warranted to all stakeholders.

CHAPTER 15

Talent

Developing Ourselves and Others—
This Is How You Win

In this chapter, I'll dig a bit deeper, from a few different perspectives, into a critical issue first mentioned in Chapter 1: talent. The issue of organizational talent sure struck a chord with everyone I interviewed, and it permeates this whole book. Every topic we discussed eventually came around to talent. In fact, it was because of my interviews that I chose to make this a dedicated chapter.

The experts I spoke with keyed in specifically on analytics talent. If the evolution from revenue management to revenue strategy is to be guided by analytics, then this evolution hinges on analytics talent. By analytics talent, I do not mean, or more precisely, I do not exclusively mean, data scientists and model builders. Tim Wiersma, founder of Revenue Generation, emphasizes that we need insightful business analysts even more than skilled modelers. Kelly McGuire, Managing Principal of Hospitality at ZS Associates, adds, "we need model builders, but we need analytically minded revenue management leaders with business acumen even more." These revenue management leaders will need to *sell* a vision for the future, and make a compelling case for certain decisions, in the context of, and even in competition with, other key needs and developments in the industry. As Kelly notes, "the need for thought leadership increases with business complexity." Revenue strategy leaders of the future will need to influence others, and in doing so, drive change, with engaging narratives grounded in analytics that are clearly articulated. I'm reminded of Albert Einstein's quote "if you can't explain it clearly, you don't understand it well enough." Sherri Kimes, Professor at National University of Singapore, believes firmly that future leaders will be grounded in analytics, but will also be able to inspire others to act via compelling communications. More succinctly, Sherri says that the future will be led by "geeks who can speak."

I believe that the best leaders in revenue management do not think of themselves as revenue management leaders; they think of themselves as *business leaders* who currently work in revenue management.

Pavan Kapur, Chief Commercial Officer at Caesars Entertainment, points out that "'analytics talent' may be too broad of a term." He sees a distinction between business analysts who interpret information to make decisions, and data scientists who can build predictive models. There may be some overlap between the two, but they are largely different skillsets, and often different people.

Where will our future talent come from? There's no clear answer to that. I've visited perhaps 15 different colleges and universities over the years to talk about revenue management, among other topics. A common question I get is "what type of background are you looking for in new hires?" More broadly, should we as an industry be looking for hospitality majors? Data analysts? Financial analysts? Students with retail, operations, or customer service experience? The answer is: all of them! My usual response in a classroom setting where I've just finished a talk on revenue management goes something like this: "I've just talked about revenue management for an hour. Do you find the topic inherently interesting? If so, then I want to hire you." That same principle applies to any hire at any level. If you have a frame of mind where you find this discipline really interesting, you are likely to be very good at it (as an aside, this is true more broadly for any discipline or industry). Some of the best revenue management leaders I've ever worked with don't come from a background that *on paper* suggests that they'd be great at revenue management, and this also is true at all levels, including bosses I've had. Brian Berry, Executive VP, Commercial Strategy, Pyramid Hotel Group, noted that the most important attribute in this discipline is *intellectual curiosity*. Both Sloan Dean, CEO of Remington Hotels, and Klaus Kohlmayr, Chief Evangelist and Head of Strategy, IDeaS Revenue Management Solutions, emphasized, however, that some particular skillsets are required as people progress in the discipline; specifically, they both noted that a grounding in micro-economics is essential, whether through on-the-job learning or more formal education. Jason Bryant, Cofounder and CEO, Nor1, says that "every revenue manager needs to be a data analyst—not just Excel but also coding, data query, and visualization as well."

Communication skills are critical of course. Regardless of how smart and talented you are, you will need to be able to convey a message, and convince others to do things, or else your impact will be limited. Trevor Stuart-Hill, President of Revenue Matters, talked about the increasing need for emotional intelligence and strategic thinking for the leaders of tomorrow. He cautions discipline practitioners "if you're all about tactics, you're about to lose your job."

In the course of my interviews, I asked a few of the experts about industry–academia partnerships, as a way of developing talent, accessing talent, and solving some problems in the process. Given my own recent transition from industry to academia, I find this topic intriguing. I believe this is an area of opportunity for the discipline of revenue management, and for the industry overall. To oversimplify a bit, there are a lot of interesting problems out there, and a lot of really smart researchers who like to take on interesting problems. That seems like it would be a good match. And yet … why aren't we seeing more such collaboration? There must be some practical impediments. This hasn't really been a priority for the corporate world, with only a few exceptions. For a productive partnership, an industry practitioner would need to devote significant time to build a relationship with an academic, likely meaning a professor or graduate student. But that industry practitioner likely has a list of short-term deliverables and is also likely to change jobs frequently. The academic too has competing priorities and may not have the latitude to accommodate the constantly shifting timelines of the corporate world. And if some partnership led to interesting results, the academic may wish to publish those findings, negating a competitive advantage. This is a clear case of what economists call the *free rider problem*. So, we're stuck. Or perhaps not. All of these impediments can be addressed. There are so many opportunities for industry-level research that could benefit the whole industry. As a simple example, are there pricing strategies that would help avoid certain types of price wars? If so, this would benefit the entire industry (though perhaps not consumers). Or, are there certain types of data sources that prove useful in forecasting demand, or upsell propensity, or cancellations, or anything else? This too would benefit the entire industry. And of course, there are problems that would be specific to a company, for example, a pricing model for multiyear groups or an inventory model for outlets, or customer-centric revenue management; these could be set up as simple paid consulting arrangements (full disclosure: I am not pitching myself here; my lifelong loyalty to Marriott would likely preclude me from any such engagements). I've met a lot of very smart researchers over the years, some of whom I interviewed for this book, and I'm certain there are a lot of complex problems to solve; this remains, for now, a largely untapped opportunity.

I'd like to end this chapter with a note on learning. As noted in Chapter 1, a learning culture is a requirement for success, and this of course goes well beyond revenue management and revenue strategy. And it goes well beyond training too. For example, training on a system that teaches us how to do certain things is of limited value without the larger context of why you may or may not want to do those things. At the risk of sounding like an academic, I believe that the *half-life* of formal education declines as business complexity increases; given that this is our trajectory for the foreseeable future, a cadence and habit of lifelong learning will only increase in importance. In fact, the evolution to revenue strategy requires it. Individuals with this learning mindset will be the ones to shape the future, and companies that recognize this and act on it will be the ones that win.

CHAPTER 16

Thoughts for the Future

The Road to Revenue Strategy

If you've read this far, I thank you for your interest and commitment! As noted in the introduction, this great discipline is my professional passion, and I hope that has become obvious to the reader. The industry and academic experts I interviewed for this book also share that passion.

We have covered a lot in this book. We began with an assessment of the current state of revenue management, and then set the context for the evolution to revenue strategy. We took another look at the five topics I presented in the HSMAI conference: forecasting, pricing, THRM, analytics and talent. And we discussed how the evolution to revenue strategy has other key components as well, such as loyalty, distribution, merchandising, machine learning, and managing through economic cycles. I won't do any sort of recap here; rather, I'd like to weave some concepts together and paint a picture of the future, from my own perspective as well as those of the many experts I interviewed.

Where are we headed? Well, we've seen a few themes in the preceding chapters. The overriding theme of course is that revenue management will continue to evolve into revenue strategy. This means that the discipline itself will become much broader in scope, and incorporate more demand generation and demand capture, in addition to demand management. The foundations of forecasting, inventory management, and pricing will certainly remain critical. However, they will increasingly be driven by technology, specifically modeling and automation, both of which will be fed with a wider range of data sources, and powered by machine learning.

The role of a revenue manager, then, will evolve too. As technology supports more of the tactics, revenue managers will either cover more hotels, or take on a more strategic role, or both. Especially for more complex hotels, and certainly for larger sets of hotels, including brands and portfolios, the role of a revenue manager will evolve into a revenue strategist. At its core, this means a business strategist who is leading decisions across all revenue streams and through all phases of the customer funnel. These revenue strategists will also remain the primary source for, and interpreter of, topline performance metrics, a role whose importance will only increase.

In the early stages, this evolution will entail a more strategic perspective on revenue management. We could call this strategic revenue management. This entails making pricing and inventory decisions that are more than *merely* tactical. As discussed in Chapter 8, such decisions are likely to involve distribution and loyalty. Strategic revenue management will also include pricing and inventory decisions related to customer acquisition and retention. Cindy Estis Green, CEO and Cofounder of Kalibri Labs, points out that, in many cases, a focus on channel controls and loyalty may have a higher marginal return than a focus on *traditional revenue management*. There is of course upside in improving our pricing, both the modeling and the execution. However, Cindy notes that "pricing is only one of the many levers available to a commercial team," and that "commercial strategy is an emerging discipline that expands upon the longstanding revenue management approach to go beyond smart pricing and inventory controls." For example, taking a holistic view that includes acquisition, loyalty, channel costs, and segment mix, and then managing to *Net Revenue,* and a corresponding *Net RPI,* will lead to different decisions, including investment decisions, than managing to RPI.

Revenue strategy, however, goes beyond strategic revenue management, because revenue strategy goes well beyond forecasting, pricing, and inventory decisions. The revenue strategists of the future will be involved in all revenue generation decisions, covering the spectrum from marketing spend to branding initiatives, and from cancellation and change policies to goal-setting, and much more. Revenue strategists will need to drive decisions on merchandising, not just display and presentation, but also a *shopping cart* approach with room attributes and other add-ons. A few companies are well down this path already, but much work remains. Certainly, executing these types of decisions requires significant automation in the tactical areas of revenue management, meaning forecasting, pricing, and inventory management. Revenue strategists will also be involved in personalization efforts, from targeted marketing to bundling/packaging to aspects of the on-property experience, with a keen focus on specific goals and associated metrics. Revenue strategists will drive decisions throughout industry cycles, including risk management, scenario planning, and even tradeoffs between short- and long-term objectives. Such decisions could involve brand standards, loyalty thresholds, technology investments, and much more. Revenue strategists will even shape decisions on how hotels can/should compete with alternative lodging.

Taking a holistic view, Bob Cross, Chairman of Revenue Analytics, emphasizes that "humans should be *primarily* focused on strategy." He adds that revenue strategists of the future should be asking and answering questions such as "what should our goals be?" and "how should we position ourselves to achieve those goals?" This, then, is the essence of revenue strategy: determine what we would like to achieve, set metrics and goals that move us in that direction, figure out what actions and allocation of limited resources will influence those metrics, measure and communicate progress, adjust and repeat! The *adjust* part, however, seems to cause a great deal of angst. We have assumptions about how specific actions and resource allocations will influence outcomes, but we don't really know until we try. The evolution to revenue strategy will require a never-ending series of controlled experiments to determine what is working. Let me offer an analogy: there is a saying in some martial arts circles that "you either win or you learn." I believe this is applicable to revenue strategy, and more broadly, to business strategy.

As noted in Chapter 1, Sloan Dean, CEO of Remington Hotels, describes an organizational approach to achieving this in terms of commercial services, painting the picture of an organization that includes commercial services leaders at all levels; for example, we'll see titles like "Area Director of Commercial Services." And Sloan notes that these positions will require soft skills such as communication, leadership, and emotional intelligence, in addition to a significant grounding in analytics.

The evolution to revenue strategy doesn't just happen on its own; rather it happens as a direct result of actions taken by individuals, and each of us plays a role. With that in mind, I challenge each reader of this book to pick one topic of interest (or a whole chapter) and commit to making meaningful improvement in that area in the next 12 months, for yourself and your stakeholders; if you can compress the timeline, or address more than one topic, you earn extra credit ☺.

The opportunities to elevate this discipline are almost boundless. Those leaders that embrace change, individually and collectively, and those that can *get comfortable being uncomfortable* will be well positioned for success. My hope is that each of us can contribute in unique and meaningful ways to make this great discipline even greater, and that you, the reader, continue to learn and get better at your craft, and in doing so, raise the bar for others.

I'll close with one of my favorite quotes, this one from Maya Angelou:

> Courage is the most important of all the virtues . . . because without courage, you can't practice any other virtue.

May you have the courage to make a significant difference, in this discipline, in the industry, and in the lives of those around you.

Appendices

Appendix 1

	Price	Population Demand	Professor Demand	Population Revenue	Professor Revenue
	$ 150	500	150	$ 75,000	$ 22,500
	$ 149	515	172	$ 76,728	$ 25,668
Change	–0.7%	3.0%	14.8%	2.3%	14.1%

Figure A1.1 shows a hypothetical example of a price decrease and the impact on the overall population versus the impact on college professors

This appendix is referenced in Chapter 6. This example shows a scenario where the college professors are more price-sensitive, meaning their demand is more price elastic, than the overall population.

Appendix 2

The following table shows the figures that are referenced in Chapter 14:

Hotel#	This Year Revenue	Last Year Revenue	Dollar Change	Percent Change
1	$28.26	$20.56	$7.70	37%
2	$13.83	$17.71	$(3.88)	−22%
3	$8.97	$20.73	$(11.76)	−57%
4	$5.49	$19.85	$(14.36)	−72%
5	$10.11	$17.61	$(7.50)	−43%
6	$12.84	$22.88	$(10.04)	−44%
7	$26.62	$20.80	$5.82	28%
8	$9.38	$17.90	$(8.52)	−48%
9	$41.69	$22.07	$19.62	89%
10	$32.46	$18.19	$14.27	78%
11	$23.39	$19.11	$4.28	22%
12	$12.39	$21.30	$(8.91)	−42%
13	$8.84	$22.71	$(13.86)	−61%
14	$10.72	$18.98	$(8.26)	−44%
15	$27.31	$22.46	$4.85	22%
16	$13.62	$18.99	$(5.37)	−28%
17	$16.29	$19.69	$(3.39)	−17%
18	$13.31	$21.16	$(7.85)	−37%
19	$23.43	$17.25	$6.18	36%
20	$33.27	$20.25	$13.01	64%
Total	$372.22	$400.22	$(28.00)	−7%

Figure A2.1 Revenue vs Last Year, by hotel and aggregate

Appendix 3

In Chapter 5, I note that a *win–loss model* can be used for groups, but is much more difficult for retail. When quoting group rates to a customer, we can record when the customer says yes or no, and the corresponding rate (e.g., one customer said yes to a room rate of $229; another said no to a room rate of $299). Several caveats apply here. Each of these room rate quotes is in the context of other parameters of the group or hotel or offer, such as meeting space charges, catering expectations, concessions, commissions, and much more. Additionally, data quality matters a lot here. For example, the rate recorded as a *no* needs to represent what the customer actually said no to (as opposed to, for example, their proposed rate, or a hotel's break-even rate). The reason all of this is more difficult for retail rates is largely because retail rates are public. We know what the customer says *yes* to, because they book it. But we don't know what they say *no* to, because we are not sure what they have seen, or if they are just shopping. This is why, these retail models are often called *win-only models* (because we don't know the *losses*).

Additional Resources

- HSMAI ROC: Hotel Sales and Marketing Revenue Optimization Conference
- *Attribute Smoothing—A Pattern Forecasting Technique*, published in 1998.
- Marriott Edelman Award writeup: see Informs.org.
- *A/B Testing is the Tricycle of Analytics*, Mike Lukianoff
- *Bringing Order to Discounts Gone Haywire*, Bain & Company
- *Freakonomics*, Stephen J. Dubner and Steven D. Levitt
- *Total Hotel Revenue Management: Why Aren't We Better at This?*, Sheryl Kimes and Dave Roberts, on www.hospitalitynet.org
- *IDeaS Unconstrained Conversations* podcast series

About the Author

Dave Roberts, In August 2020, Dave began teaching in the Nolan School of Hotel Administration at Cornell's SC Johnson College of Business. He teaches courses in Hotel Operations and Channel Distribution. Prior to joining Cornell's faculty, he taught graduate courses in Business Strategy and Corporate Finance at Virginia Tech's Pamplin College of Business.

Dave retired from Marriott in 2019, after 23 years with the company. Most recently, he was the Senior Vice President of Revenue Strategy and Solutions. In this role, he was responsible for revenue management strategy and execution for over 7,000 hotels worldwide. He also led Revenue Analytics, providing topline analysis for the company, as well as sales systems, providing strategy, development, and deployment of technology to manage meeting and event business.

Prior to this role, in addition to leading revenue management, he led the Consumer Insights department, providing consumer research and analytics for regional and corporate stakeholders. Dave has also been Regional Vice President of Market Strategy for Marriott's Eastern Region, and Vice President of Global Pricing, in addition to several other roles in the company.

Prior to Marriott, Dave was a manager in the Finance Department at American Airlines, working on airplane purchases and route economics. He was also a technical consultant on missile defense for the U.S. Department of Defense, as part of the *Star Wars* initiative.

He has a BS and an MS in Operations Research from Cornell and an MBA with majors in Finance and Economics from Northwestern's Kellogg School. He holds a U.S. patent on a software product (a data matching algorithm) and has published several academic papers on such topics as forecasting, options pricing, and customer choice modeling. Dave was on IBM's Business Analytics Advisory Board for six years and on Cornell's Center for Hospitality Research Advisory Board for five years. He has been a frequent speaker at industry events, as well as several top universities. In his spare time, he enjoys martial arts and astronomy.

Index

A/B testing, 37, 51–53, 56, 104–106
aggression, 63
alternative lodging, 19, 115
analytics, 69, 109
   performance, 102–104
   topline, 5, 101–107
Anderson, C., 50, 71, 98
Artificial Intelligence (AI), 3, 96
attrition, 10, 21

benchmarking, 37–38, 79
benefit maximization, 101
Berry, B., 76, 79
Bryant, J., 74, 110
Busch, M., 68, 70, 79
business case reviews, 106–107

choice deferral, 75–76
coherent strategy, 6
college professor rate, 41–47, 51–54, 117
compset, 38
conscious parallelism, 39
constrained demand forecast, 19
COVID-19 pandemic, 3, 15, 16, 32, 41, 59, 81, 84
Cross, B., 28, 33, 46–47, 115
Cross, D., 32, 36, 74, 76, 97

Dean, S., 7–8, 70, 79, 96, 110, 115
decoy pricing, 73–76
demand-based pricing, 39–40
demand capture, 5, 113
demand forecasting, 3, 10, 15–21, 28, 32, 33, 86, 89, 92, 96
dilution, 11–14, 41, 104
discount audit, 92
discounted rates, 13, 41–42, 68, 70, 92
   A/B testing, 52–53
   incremental *vs.* tradedown, 43–46

   mix *vs.* yield, 56–57
   opaque rates, 50–51
   price discrimination and screening, 47–50
   repeat behavior, 53–55
   success, measuring, 51
discount war, 85
displacement, 11–14
displacement simulation, 62
distribution, 67–71
dynamic pricing, 64–66

Einstein, A., 38
Eister, C., 36, 76, 98

fenced rate, 47
Florida Resident Rate, 55
forecasting, 3, 15, 96, 114
   absolute *vs.* bias, 18, 21
   demand, 3, 10, 15–21, 28, 32, 33, 86, 89, 92, 96
   system error *vs.* user error, 18–19
free rider problem, 37, 111

goal setting, 107, 114
Green, C. E., 6, 57, 84, 114
grouping up, 86, 87
Group Pricing Optimizer (GPO), 35
group up strategy, 86, 87
group wash, 21

half-life, 112
happy/sad litmus test, 69, 102, 103
hospitality, 7, 9, 11, 49, 57, 74, 75, 77, 78, 82, 85, 98, 103–106
Hotel Sales and Marketing Association International Revenue Optimization Conference (HSMAI ROC), 1, 2, 8, 83, 113

incrementality, 20, 47, 51–57
influencing behavior, 68
inventory management
   caution on, 25–26
   component, 11
   decisions, 87, 93
   problem, 24, 25
inventory risks, 92

Jankowski, E., 102

Kalibri Vision, 104
Kapur, P., 69–70, 110
Kimes, S., 77–79, 82, 85, 109–110
Kohlmayr, K., 31, 86, 110

last room availability (LRA), 36, 59–63
loyalty, 67–71
Lukianoff, M., 52

McGuire, K., 17, 78, 109
machine learning, 20, 21, 95–100, 113
member offers, 67, 68
member rates, 67
merchandising
   choice deferral, 75–76
   decoy pricing, 73–76
   machine learning and, 98
multivariate testing, 53

negotiated account rates, 35, 59
   cheaters, 63–64
   dynamic pricing, 64–66
   last room availability, 59–63
Nicolau, J., 74

one yield system, 34
onward distribution, 70
opaque rates, 50–51
optimal channel mix, 26
optimal mix, 26
optimization. *See* price optimization
overall population, 42, 117
overriding, 32–34

Paradox of Choice, The (Schwartz), 75
partly cancel, 21
performance analytics, 102–104
postmortems, 106
preferred availability, 69
previous downturn (2009), 84
price discrimination, 47–48
price modeling, 28
price optimization, 3–4, 10, 11, 27, 28
price-sensitive forecast, 20
pricing, 3–4, 10, 27–30
   adoption, 30–34
   benchmarking and, 37–38
   competitive response, 38–39
   decoy, 73–76
   demand, 29, 39–40
   dynamic, 64–66
   and inventory, 3, 5, 6, 9, 10, 15, 17, 18, 20–22, 67, 70, 71, 87, 92, 97, 101, 114
   machine learning for, 97
   objectives, 37
   retail model, 34–36
prisoner's dilemma, 83

qualified rate, 47

rate risks, 92
reference pricing, 83
regret anticipation, 75
reinforcement models, 96
restrictions, 23
revenue management, 9
   in downturn, 81–90
   in recovery, 91–93
   value of TM, 87–90
revenue management system (RMS), 3, 4, 16, 18, 19, 27, 28, 89, 96
revenue manager, 2, 5, 7, 10, 11, 16, 17, 22, 27, 28, 31–33, 39, 52, 60, 82, 98, 101, 102, 110, 113, 114
Revenue Per Available Room (RevPAR), 3, 40, 81, 84, 91, 104

revenue strategy, 113–116
evolution to, 1–8
revenue vs last year, 103, 118
RevPAR Index (RPI), 7
Rubinacci, A., 78, 104

Schwartz, B., 75
screening, 48–50
semi-supervised models, 96
shopping cart approach, 114
slippage, 21
squatter rates, 36
S-shaped price response function, 88
strategy, 1, 6
STR data, 37
Stuart-Hill, T., 9, 70, 111
Sunday fallacy, 90
supervised models, 96
supply forecast, 10

talent, 5, 109–112
time-series forecast, 89
topline analytics, 5, 101–107
total hotel revenue management (THRM), 4, 77–79
total hotel revenue optimization (THRO), 77
traditional revenue management, 114

unconscious bias, 106
undisciplined discounting, 47
unsupervised models, 96

Wiersma, T., 32, 109
win–loss models, 35, 119
win-only models, 35, 119

Yield Management, 9

OTHER TITLES IN THE TOURISM AND HOSPITALITY MANAGEMENT COLLECTION

Betsy Bender Stringam, New Mexico State University, Editor

- *Astrotourism* by Michael Marlin
- *Enhancing Joy in Travel* by Murphy-Berman Virginia
- *Healthy Vines, Pure Wines* by Pamela Lanier and Jessica Nicole Hughes
- *Overtourism* by Helene von Magius Møgelhøj
- *Food and Beverage Management in the Luxury Hotel Industry* by Sylvain Boussard
- *Targeting the Mature Traveler* by Jacqueline Jeynes
- *Hospitality* by Chris Sheppardson
- *Food and Architecture* by Subhadip Majumder and Sounak Majumder
- *A Time of Change in Hospitality Leadership* by Chris Sheppardson

Concise and Applied Business Books

The Collection listed above is one of 30 business subject collections that Business Expert Press has grown to make BEP a premiere publisher of print and digital books. Our concise and applied books are for...

- Professionals and Practitioners
- Faculty who adopt our books for courses
- Librarians who know that BEP's Digital Libraries are a unique way to offer students ebooks to download, not restricted with any digital rights management
- Executive Training Course Leaders
- Business Seminar Organizers

Business Expert Press books are for anyone who needs to dig deeper on business ideas, goals, and solutions to everyday problems. Whether one print book, one ebook, or buying a digital library of 110 ebooks, we remain the affordable and smart way to be business smart. For more information, please visit www.businessexpertpress.com, or contact sales@businessexpertpress.com.

CPSIA information can be obtained
at www.ICGtesting.com
Printed in the USA
LVHW021114130222
710994LV00015B/1370